WHAT PARENTS ARE SAYING ABOUT *TODDLER SING & SIGN*

"Wow! *Toddler Sing & Sign* is so much fun. Toddlers are so receptive to learning through songs and play and toys with their parents and their peers. *Toddler Sing & Sign* provides for practice, repetition, reinforcement, and celebration of new learning day in and day out. I recommend this book to all babies, parents, and families."

—JONI C.

"My one-, two-, and four-year-old children love the *Toddler Sing & Sign* CD. Even my 13-year-old enjoys singing and signing with his brother and sisters."

—CYNDI K.

"I am using my *Baby Sing & Sign* book with our new son, but his older brother loves his *Toddler Sing & Sign* program. He enjoys singing along and doing some of the signs. He will sign with his verbal language when he REALLY wants to get his point across. We're eager for the new baby to start signing with us. Singing and signing is a family act at our house!"

—HEATHER G.

"Understanding your child and having your child understand you at such an early age is truly a mind-blowing thing. It builds a powerful bond. We started the *Baby Sing & Sign* program because we understood that children who learn to sign are able to express their basic needs and may even do better in school. Now a toddler, our daughter loves *Toddler Sing & Sign*. She is very verbal but still uses her signs, and she is helping us to teach her baby brother to sign—giving him the gift of communication with his family."

—ALAN L.

"I am a music therapist and mom to children ages one and three years. I put this book to work in both my special education classroom and my home. My children love the songs and the signs. I get frequent requests at school and at home for *Toddler Sing & Sign* songs, signs, and activities."

—ANGELA W.

"I knew from the day my daughter was born that I would establish multiple ways to communicate with her. I wanted to teach my daughter baby sign language to jump-start her ability to tell us her wants and needs. Now two years old, she still relies on both spoken and signed words in order to communicate. Our pediatrician remarked that her language skills were exceptional. She expresses herself well and adores her 'Miller' music."
—JONANN E.

"I love the toys and games! There are so many creative ideas and it really helped me to start thinking 'outside of the box' of play activities for fun and learning. The mixture of engaging music with sign language learning is wonderful. I also loved the way you show how a child might perform the signs, as well as their ASL version. I probably would not have realized my son was actually signing for me without your help."
—AARON F.

"We own many CDs of children's music. I can't stress enough how engaging the *Toddler Sing & Sign* CD is for our daughter! The songs truly capture her attention, her imagination, and her heart. She loves to 'be' the animals she sings about and insists I join her and sing her favorite 'Turtle' and 'Rooster' tunes. She will sign and say 'more' to hear those two again and again. The repetition the music provides has helped her improve her ability to say many of the lyrics of the songs. We love *Toddler Sing & Sign*!"
—BARBIE G.

"I attribute my child's great verbal skills to *Baby Sing & Sign*. We loved the book and enjoyed all the activities with our son from a very early age. *Toddler Sing & Sign* is the perfect 'next step' for our son as he continues to learn and grow with Anne's songs, signs, and games."
—VICKIE T.

"I am thrilled that *Toddler Sing & Sign* is an ASL-based program. I want my child to learn sign language as a second language so that as she grows, she can communicate with children who need to sign to communicate because they are deaf or cannot speak. The songs and activities were wonderful and easy to enjoy at home. I also gave a copy of this book to my daycare provider, and now she is *Toddler Sing & Sign*-ing with all the children she cares for."
—SAM C.

"Combining singing, signing, movement, play materials, and picture books keeps my toddler interested and happy—and she stays in one place for longer than 30 seconds! This is a miracle in and of itself. What a wonderful learning experience for our family. You provided new ways for me to communicate with my child and stimulate her growing brain."
—LAUREN M.

TODDLER
SING & SIGN®

ANNE MEEKER MILLER, PhD

TODDLER SING & SIGN®

Improve Your Child's Vocabulary and Verbal Skills

the Fun Way through Music and Play

Marlowe and Company
New York

Toddler Sing & Sign:
Improve Your Child's Vocabulary and Verbal Skills the Fun Way through Music and Play

Copyright © 2007 by Anne Meeker Miller.

Published by
Marlowe & Company
An Imprint of Avalon Publishing Group, Incorporated
245 West 17th Street • 11th Floor
New York, NY 10011–5300

AVALON
publishing group incorporated

A portion of the proceeds from the sale of this book goes to nonprofit organizations that support children's causes in the Kansas City area.

Library of Congress Cataloging-in-Publication Data is available.

ISBN-13: 978–1-60094–020–0
ISBN-10: 1–60094–020-X

9 8 7 6 5 4 3 2 1

Designed by *Pauline Neuwirth, Neuwirth and Associates*
Printed in the United States of America

For Marjorie Gamble Lamb,
my fairy godmother
(1920–2005)

CONTENTS

FOREWORD

—BY JIM COSCOVE

Children know all about rhythm. They're closer to it than we are. Not so long ago they were floating in wombs that thumped with the rhythm of their mothers' hearts—the rhythm of safety and comfort. And as our children become more familiar with their own beat, they discover their spirits and their voices.

When we harness that rhythm by talking, reading, and singing with our children, we provide them the developmental building blocks for success in language, math, and life in general. And I happen to think that music is the key. It works like megavitamins for our brains—stimulating cells and helping us make connections.

In *Toddler Sing & Sign*, Anne Meeker Miller has coupled music (and her angelic voice) with science and the art of sign language to help make it easier to communicate with our kids.

A mountain of research has proven that music helps stimulate a child's cognitive, social, and physical development. And it's great for spiritual development, too. Music moves us. It nips at our spirits. It inspires us. It evokes emotion. That's how it works to help us learn.

I must admit that I dismissed the idea of teaching "signs" to infants and toddlers as a bit of trendy "psycho-babble." But I fell in love with the process. It's simple and it works. When my wife and I taught our daughter the sign for "more," the communication floodgates opened. That one simple sign triggered in her (and equally as important in us) the realization that we can all get what we want and need when we're clear about it.

As our little girl made the transition to feeding herself, potty training, and a "big girl" bed, her verbal skills improved exponentially, but sometimes she became frustrated trying to find the right words. That's where sign language comes in handy.

Little toddler minds are so full of new stimuli and they get so excited to talk, that sometimes they struggle with words, or all the sounds get jumbled in their mouths and come out at the same time. *Toddler Sing & Sign* has helped make the transition smoother.

You hold in your hands a valuable teaching tool—one of many tools we have at our disposal. And as we grow as parents we soon find that we need as many tools as we can get to help navigate our children's (and our own) developmental stages.

Perhaps the best tools a parent has are a comforting voice, a gentle touch, and an encouraging interaction with a child. Put all those tools to work and watch the rhythm of communication unfold.

Jim Cosgrove, better known as "Mr. Stinky Feet," is an award-winning children's entertainer, Warner Brothers recording artist, and grateful father of two.

INTRODUCTION

"Children are all foreigners."
—RALPH WALDO EMERSON (1803-1882)

"What would you like for breakfast, my little boy?"

"Babubas snickly-snoo," Greg said with the conviction of one who knows exactly what food sounds delicious.

"I am sorry, Greg, but Mommy doesn't know what you are saying. What does 'babubas snickly-snoo' look like? Where do we store it in the kitchen?"

Greg's face began to redden as his words grew louder and more adamant: "Babubas snickly-snoo, *babubas snickly-snoo*, BABUBAS SNICKLY-SNOO!"

I can't be certain, but I believe my toddler son Greg spoke perfect Latin or some other ancient, foreign dialect during his second year of life. His articulation and inflection were passionate and precise, and he paused intelligently at the end of his Latin sentences, waiting with bated baby-boy breath for a proper reply from me. I would have sold my Little Tykes Crazy Coupe for just a glimpse into the frenzied language processing going on in his head.

I tried to achieve an "I have no idea what you are saying, but I will pretend I do" level of banter with my son, but he was not easily bamboozled. In addition to being conversant in Latin, Greg could smell an imposter. And judging by his wailing that usually followed, I was terribly inefficient when it came to translating his utterances into action in order to satisfy his laundry list of wants and needs.

Compounding this predicament was the acceleration of Greg's gross-motor skills. Those are the large-muscle movements a child uses to walk, run, and climb onto your kitchen counter in order to pour herself a tall, breakable glass of apple juice. "Gross" is actually an apt descriptor for this newfound toddler ability to move from place to place in your house, at the mall, or off down the street while you are folding laundry. And as toddlers begin to locomote, the lure of the "open road" is often too delicious for them to resist. Most parents need to revisit their childproofing measures to make sure that their toddler can't travel too far without adult supervision.

In my first book, *Baby Sing & Sign,* I created a sign language communication program that provides numerous developmental benefits for babies and is tons of fun for the entire family. Through music and play activities, parents can teach their infants key signs from *American Sign Language (ASL),* the language commonly used by the deaf community. With their baby safely perched in their lap, a high chair, or baby bouncer, parents and caregivers can sing and sign with zeal as their infants gaze adoringly at their fascinating and expressive adult faces. In turn, babies learn to use these signs to communicate their needs—for example, MORE, HUG, or ALL DONE.

Even after children begin to utter their first words, signing continues to benefit toddlers.

- Sign language helps parents understand words that are not clearly articulated when their toddler signs as well as speaks a word.
- Sign language is a visual representation of spoken words, helping toddlers master new words that represent feelings or ideas.
- Signs also help toddlers retrieve words from their memory that are familiar but may be temporarily forgotten. For instance, the child may not recall how to say "elephant" but can perform the sign. Seeing her own hands form the elephant's trunk triggers her memory of how to speak the word "elephant."
- Sign language helps toddlers when they are tired or too frustrated to communicate quickly and clearly, thus heading off temper tantrums and meltdowns.

Once your child is a confident walker and on the move, it is difficult to get "face time" with her for sign language teaching and practice. Toddlers are little people with places to go, things to do, and people to meet. I know parents who have grown fairly proficient at signing in front of their toddlers while running backward. How, then, do we continue to support a toddler's emerging verbal skills as she focuses her considerable energy on her body in motion?

The stakes become higher once she can maneuver herself to get to the places and things she desires. I watched one toddler climb pantry shelves like a little spider monkey to grab a box of Grammy Bears from the very tippy-top before shimmying back down again. If a toddler's parent or caregiver can't figure out what she is communicating through sign or speech, she may well be able to take matters into her own little hands.

I created *Toddler Sing & Sign* specifically for the needs of one- and two-year-old children. Through songs, games, picture books, and a hefty dose of affection, you can help build the emerging language and literacy skills of your toddler. Signs for animals and colors are the focus of this book; animals are interesting and motivating for toddlers to sign, and children of this age are beginning to be able to label and sort objects by color. As with the *Baby Sing & Sign* program, I include functional vocabulary to help toddlers continue to communicate their wants and needs with both their spoken and signed words. The *Toddler Sing & Sign* program was developed in response to the demand of families in the Kansas City area who participated in *Baby Sing & Sign* classes. They wanted continued experiences in music, sign language, and play that addressed the developmental needs of their toddlers. Because sign language has received continued media coverage as a viable method for communicating with preverbal infants and toddlers, most parents I meet are sold on the idea; what they are lacking is a set of easy strategies to engage their child in sign language learning. *Toddler Sing & Sign* requires no special training or equipment. All that is necessary is a willingness to sing, sign, and play one page and one day at a time, and to have fun and enhance the bond you share with your child in the process.

I've said it before and I will say it again: parenting is not for wimps. But I believe in you and your ability to navigate this bumpy toddler terrain with courage and humor (and a box of Bob the Builder bandages for your toddler's tender knees and elbows).

So here we go!

WHY SIGN?

We have learned that babies can learn to communicate their wants and needs using gestures long before their vocal mechanisms are mature enough to verbalize. In groundbreaking research, child psychologists Linda Acredolo and Susan Goodwyn found that using sign language with children at an early age supports the natural development of their ability to speak. Babies who learn to sign experience less frustration and often verbalize sooner than their peers, and most importantly, sign language strengthens the bond between caregiver and child. Acredolo and Goodwyn's "baby signs" are gestures they invented or modified from American Sign Language to best fit the hand-shape development of babies.

♪ The Benefitsof Teaching American Sign Language to Toddlers and Preschoolers

In my *Sing & Sign* programs I advocate the use of American Sign Language (ASL), the widely accepted system of signed communication for the deaf. The ASL hand shapes often form "pictures" of the objects or ideas they represent and are therefore simple for the child to learn. For instance, the sign for EAT is performed by tapping gathered fingertips to the lips, pantomiming the act of eating food. This is an obvious and logical gesture for a hungry toddler who wants a snack. As interest and enthusiasm for sign language with infants and toddlers continues to grow, there is a trend to utilize ASL or ASL-based gestures or "real signs" to communicate with preverbal babies and toddlers.

The benefit of ASL for babies as a prelude to spoken language has been well documented. We also know there is a great deal of difference between children under the age of two in terms of when they first begin to express themselves with spoken words. Some toddlers may be well on their way in their journey toward mastery of speech, but still rely on signing to communicate words they are not able to articulate clearly. However, in addition to the use of sign as an alternative to speech, there are many benefits to continued use of ASL with toddlers as well as preschoolers. Some of these benefits are:

1. **Signing builds a child's vocabulary.** The act of signing helps children store and retrieve words in their "motor memory." By performing the sign with their hands, they are more likely to remember the word in combination with its meaning. A frustrated toddler may be saying many words clearly; however, when she is tired or frustrated, she may revert to signing PLEASE to get a drink of water or a hug. The act of signing PLEASE will likely help the child to remember both the spoken word PLEASE and its meaning. Sign language can also be used to teach children to manipulate letters and sounds—the building blocks of reading and writing.

2. **Signing helps develop fine and gross motor skills.** Children practice their fine-motor (finger motions) and gross-motor (walk, hop, dance) movement as they imitate and perform signs.

3. **Signing is fun.** Children love to sign with their families or playmates. It can continue to be a special "love language" with parents and caring adults long after children have learned to speak. Older siblings can be the best sign language teachers for their baby brothers or sisters. When paired with

music and play, sign language is enjoyable and a great way to connect with others.

4. **Signing ASL offers a second language.** Mastering sign language at an early age may enable children to use their signing skills with peers who are hearing impaired or deaf. Families who adopt children internationally find that sign language can be an immediate communication tool for bridging the distance between spoken English and the child's native language.

5. **Signing provides an integrated sensory experience.** Carol Stock Kranowitz, a noted expert on sensory integration dysfunction and author of *The Out-of-Sync Child* (Perigee), describes the brain as a sensory processing machine. It modulates or balances all the information we receive from our senses: sight, hearing, touch, smell, and taste. According to Kranowitz, "In a swift neurological process, your brain analyzes, organizes, and connects—i.e., integrates—them." A sensory-rich environment filled with interesting play materials, books, and music helps children learn to receive and organize sensory information. Signing combines sensory experiences as gestures are "felt" with the fingers and seen by the child who signs or observes the signing of others. *Toddler Sing & Sign* provides multiple sensory benefits to children.

♪ What Science Says about Singing and Signing

For those who are interested in findings from the scientific community regarding sign language instruction and music in the lives of young children, here are a few excerpts from some notable research studies:

○ Kay Rush researched the benefits of using sign language to enhance literacy and language concepts with preschoolers and found that signing helps build language connections in the brain. She states: "Signing is a kinetic act that stimulates activity in both the right brain, which is responsible for visual-spatial reasoning and long-term memory, and the left brain, which is responsible for processing language. When you are signing with hearing children, you are not only reinforcing their existing language, you are also giving them another way to express a concept they already know, thus creating another connection to that information in their brain."

Rush notes that preschoolers who use sign language scored better on vocabulary tests and attained higher reading levels than their nonsigning peers.

○ Ursula Hildebrandt, a researcher at the University of Washington, found that hearing infants preferred sign language to pantomime. Hildebrandt says: "Infants seem to be set up to pay attention to language at birth and we've seen they have a remarkable sensitivity to spoken language. This work is important because it broadens this bias to include an unfamiliar language in a completely unique modality."

○ Scientists at the University of California at Irvine found that musical training improves the brain's ability to process tasks having to do with space and time. Dr. Frances Rauscher writes: "By demonstrating that music improves the intellectual functioning of all children, we have shown that music education is essential for optimal cognitive development. If we do not provide adequate opportunities for our children to learn and participate in music, we are depriving them of a great resource. . . . This work does not diminish music as an art, but rather it increases the status of music as an educational tool."

THE *TODDLER SING & SIGN* PROGRAM

Toddler Sing & Sign is a unique approach to teaching sign language and is ideal for busy families. The program uses music, pictures, games, and picture books to help you and your toddler learn and practice a variety of simple and essential words from American Sign Language that can be used in meaningful communication.

The method is an outgrowth of my work as a music therapist for a public school system in the Kansas City area. Several years ago a colleague asked me about exploring the use of music as a way to help infants and toddlers learn to sign. I wrote some child-friendly songs with lyrics that focused on key words, such as MORE, PLEASE, ALL DONE, and EAT, that could be signed throughout the song. I soon found that music proved to be an incredibly engaging and motivating tool for learning sign language. Not only were babies responsive, but both they and their parents were also having fun! The result was my first book, *Baby Sing & Sign*.

Thousands of families have successfully used the *Baby Sing & Sign* program to teach their infants to sign. But babies have a way of growing up. With that reality in mind, I've developed *Toddler Sing & Sign,* the next step in a continuum of enrichment experiences to build the emerging language of one- and two-year-olds. In addition to signing, your toddler will enjoy wonderful songs, games, and activities that make possible mastery of important preliteracy skills and a love of learning.

Maggie signs HAPPY.

♪ About the Toddler Signs

The signs and words included in the book were specifically selected with toddlers in mind. Toddlers love animals: the sounds they make; the relationships between Mommy, Daddy, and baby animals; their shapes and sizes; the way they move; and the places they live. Toddlers love to point out animals they recognize in picture books, or at the park or zoo, and sign their animal names.

Toddlers also like to begin sorting and labeling things by color. They become masters at combining signs or spoken words to form short, meaningful phrases or sentences. Animal and color signs can also be combined for fun and learning. A variety of other signs are included in *Toddler Sing & Sign* that give children opportunities to observe their world and meaningfully describe their experiences, feelings, and relationships. Examples include SLOW, FAST, FRIEND, HAPPY, and SAD.

When teaching young children to sign, the gestures are often modified to better suit their fine motor capabilities. However, some parents and caregivers want to teach only true ASL signs. The reality is that a child's ability to sign depends on her development of hand shapes, starting with signs made with the whole hand and progressing to signs that require thumb or finger isolations. Children also differ in their ability to imitate fine motor movements performed by another person. This skill develops with age and experience.

Toddler Sing & Sign provides two photographs for each sign taught in the book. One shows an adult model performing the ASL sign. The second photograph shows a child performing a modification a toddler might make when he attempts to perform the ASL version of the word. It is important always to look for the child's best attempt to sign the gesture and to respond with praise. Their fine-motor skills—the small-muscle motions they can perform with their fingers—will improve over time. It is also important to give babies and toddlers objects to grasp, pick up, and manipulate to improve their dexterity and coordination.

Maia signs SLEEP.

♪ About the Toddler Songs

The ten songs included in this book and CD represent a wide variety of musical styles. Each song tells a story. The instruments and tempos are livelier than the tunes on the *Baby Sing & Sign* CD in response to a toddler's love for "moving and grooving" to songs with a beat. The two lullabies have been grouped at the end of the CD so that you can use the music as a part of your bedtime ritual if you like.

Each song on the CD provides opportunities to sing as well as sign the vocabulary included in the book. Some songs were composed for the program; others are slightly modified versions of traditional folk tunes. The melodies are simple but musically interesting to your toddler—a child can recognize and respond to the tune and rhythm, and will delight in any new verses parents and caregivers may add to extend the fun and learning. For example, your child can choose any variety of animal to sing about living on "Grandpa's Farm." Your family may want to make up new verses for creatures that could visit you as you sing "All Around the Kitchen."

When it is used as a language development program, I recommend singing these songs with toddlers for several weeks in order to give them repeated opportunities to hear and enjoy them. The tunes comprise a repertoire that can become a part of the entire family's tradition, and they are inviting to children of all ages. As with the *Baby Sing & Sign* CD, parents have shared with me that the benefit of including these songs in their family life has endured long after their children learned to speak.

With each song presented in the book, you and your child will learn new signs and practice musical as well as communication skills that are playful and *developmentally appropriate*. And don't worry—no special equipment or training is needed. *Toddler Sing & Sign* games use materials that are readily at hand and are easily incorporated into your daily routine. All that is necessary is a willingness to play and an interest in allowing your child to direct his or her learning adventure!

Gianni signs LION.

HOW TO USE THIS BOOK

This book is meant to be consumed in bite-size pieces, one song at a time.

○ Your toddler will love the CD from the start. Sing a tune with or without the CD until you know the lyrics well.

○ Once both you and your child are familiar with the song, find the signs in the corresponding song chapter and introduce them to your child.

○ The suggested games and books emphasize the signs and can be added to offer extra practice and enhance the fun as you proceed.

Toddler Sing & Sign is a process that allows you to capture your child's attention with music and teach sign language in such a playful way that children never realize they are learning new skills. The program is designed to fit into your daily life with children and is meant to enhance, rather than complicate, your daily routine.

Following a brief overview of the *Toddler Sing & Sign* program, you will find "How to Sing and Sign with Your Toddler" (page 14), which outlines the basics for teaching children how to sing and sign and illustrates the hand formations that will be used throughout the book. Answers to frequently asked questions (page 20) about sign language, music, and the unique characteristics of toddlers are also provided.

Song chapters 1 through 10—the centerpiece of the book—appear in the order of the playlist on the *Toddler Sing & Sign* music CD (found inside the back cover). Each song chapter consists of the following elements:

○ A list of the core vocabulary words being introduced. When used in combination with song, they provide a simple, fun, and natural set of signed words to accompany the music. Core words are included both in the song chapters and in the dictionary. Adult and child photograph instructions, as well as written instructions, are included for each word.

○ A list of words to review. Review words have already been included in songs and activities from previous chapters. They are included again because they naturally occur in the "song story" and because repetition helps toddlers learn.

○ A list of bonus words. Bonus words can be taught to toddlers who have already mastered the core words, and included as an extension to the play activities. They are also included for those using this program with preschoolers or primary school–age children. They are shown in the *Toddler Sing & Sign* Dictionary in the back of the book.

○ Song lyrics and musical score with guitar chords.

○ Instructions for signing each word, including written descriptions and photographs of adults and children making the signs.

○ "Tips for Introducing the Song": ideas for how to teach the song and signs listed at the beginning of the chapter as "Words to Learn."

○ "More Musical Fun": additional activities designed to extend music and sign language learning while helping to maintain the child's interest.

○ "Games and Activities": suggestions for making toys, playing games, and other activities using materials readily at hand in order to practice the sign language vocabulary. The activities can be customized to suit the developmental stage of your child and to help children grow in other areas, such as fine-motor and problem-solving skills. Homemade toys are creative and inexpensive, and playing with them also teaches your child that toys do not have to come from a store.

○ "A Sign of Success": stories that share thoughts about child development and parenting and relate the experiences of parents and other caregivers who have participated in *Toddler Sing & Sign* on their own or in classes. These vignettes are arranged in order of complexity—from a celebration of the ages and stages of "not-at-all-terrible-twos" to getting your three-year-old ready for preschool.

○ "Books to Read": recommended books for toddlers that fit the musical theme and vocabulary of a given chapter. Let this list be a starting point as you explore other titles at your local library or bookstore. Early reading experiences are important for toddlers and set the stage for their future literacy. Book engagement is an important predictor of reading success, as well as another effective way to practice sign language vocabulary.

Tabitha signs RED.

As mentioned earlier, the sign words selected for this book focus on colors and animals, along with other key signs toddlers can use in communication with others. Collectively these words and signs comprise a core vocabulary for the *Toddler Sing & Sign* program and are printed in boldface capital letters where they appear in the book.

However, there are many words listed as "bonus signs" that are embedded in the song lyrics or presented as developmentally appropriate concepts for your toddler. For instance, we sing about a BIG BEAR in the "Around the Kitchen" and "The Grizzly Bear" songs. We have included the sign for LITTLE as a bonus word so that you can talk to your child about things that are big and little. Bonus words are capitalized but not boldfaced in the chapters. These words may be of special interest to your child and may therefore be very motivating for your child to sign. You may also use this program with preschoolers and primary school–aged children, who will also welcome the challenge of signing words as they sing.

For your convenience, *Toddler Sing & Sign* includes a pictorial dictionary containing all of the signs used in the book. These pages can be duplicated so that you can keep a copy in your diaper bag or posted on your refrigerator door for quick reference. Finally, in the "References and Resources" section you will find lists of books and Web sites about language development and music for young children.

Here are some organizational features that are used throughout the book. The pronouns "he" and "she" are used alternately to refer to babies and toddlers who will use the program. Safety reminders appear in italics. The book refers to both "parents" and "caregivers" when describing caring adults who will use the program with children. Given the growing diversity of families, feel free to modify the song texts and other activities as needed to fit your family structure.

Avery signs SCARED.

♪ A Note on Homemade Toys

Each of the song chapters in *Toddler Sing & Sign* suggests games and other activities that reinforce the sign, and I sometimes suggest creating a homemade toy. When making and using homemade toys, the safety and well-being of your child are the first concerns. Please read the following points carefully before proceeding with any of the homemade toys described.

○ Homemade toys have not been subject to mandatory toy safety regulations. Please use your best judgment when preparing and playing with these items.
○ Infants and toddlers must be supervised at all times when using toys.
○ Little children put things in their mouths. Be sure toys are too large for them to choke on, are nontoxic, and have smooth surfaces.
○ As with all toys, check toys often to be certain they are safe for play.

HOW TO SING AND SIGN
WITH YOUR TODDLER

To BEGIN THE program, I suggest that you use the music CD as much as possible and sing to your child. The music is upbeat and enjoyable. Listen to the tunes in your car, during playtime, or as part of your toddler's bedtime ritual. Share your singing voice and your silliest self with your child as you dance, walk, and hop to the beat. When your child hears her "special music," she knows it is time for your undivided attention and lots of fun with you.

Once you have listened to the CD and learned the tunes, you can alternate singing with and without the CD. Singing without musical accompaniment is called *a cappella* singing. Your a cappella singing will become a source of comfort and pleasure for your child, and will create opportunities for your toddler and your entire family to make new verses and devise new games all their own.

The songs and chapters of the book are organized so that their corresponding signs are presented in a learning sequence. As you continue to enjoy the music together, take the time to read this book and practice the signs on your own. Once toddlers are able to imitate your gestures and understand that there is a connection between hand shapes and words, their sign vocabulary typically takes off. I have known children who waited six months before using their first signed word, and one week later they added twenty more signs to their conversations with others. For instruction on physically teaching the signs, see the "Hand Formations" section on page 17.

If *Toddler Sing & Sign* is your first child sign language program, I suggest you start with several signed words, such as EAT, PLAY, and MUSIC. These are motivating signs for her to get what she desires, and help her understand the connection between gestures and words. When your child first imitates the sign, she may not yet realize that her gestures actually mean something. Be patient and continue to sign and speak these words. You know your toddler best and will begin to notice her responses to your signed words. Perhaps she will smile when you say and sign the word PLAY or look toward the pantry or refrigerator when you say and sign EAT. With time and opportunities to practice, she will likely begin to use these simple signs to tell you she wants. The first time your toddler signs with purpose will be wonderful for you both!

Once your child is successful in understanding language as well as expressing herself with gesture, you can begin to add other signs that are motivating (animals, colors, foods) as well as useful (PLEASE, HELP, ALL DONE) for toddlers.

If you haven't already used it—and even if you have—the *Baby Sing & Sign* book would be a helpful resource for you as you begin the process of teaching your child to sign words with music, play, and picture books. It contains instructions for teaching more than forty practical and helpful signs, and the companion music CD is great for children of all ages.

Maia signs DADDY.

SPEECH DEVELOPMENT

Continue to speak when you sign. The goal of teaching babies and toddlers sign language is to support the development of their emerging speech. You are giving them the opportunity to "flex their language muscles" as their vocal mechanism and language processing skills develop, so it is essential that you combine speech with gesture.

Parents often worry about what to expect regarding their child's development of speech. *When should my child be talking? How many words should she be saying and how often?* This is particularly true when their first- or second-born child provides a point of comparison for their baby's language skills. Perhaps big brother or sister talked sooner or more often than the new baby. Most experts agree that, in general, first-born and girl babies are the earliest to talk, and there is a wide range of what is considered to be normal language development in children.

Parents should also pay attention not only to what infants and toddlers express through sign language and speech, but also to how well the child understands and responds to what others say to her. ("Where is the monkey on the page of our book? Point to the monkey in the picture.") The American Academy of Pediatrics suggests that by twenty-four months, toddlers should be able to combine two or three spoken words into sentences. They should also be able to follow simple instructions and repeat words they hear in conversation.

This book will help you create activities that you can enjoy with your child while connecting with her in a more meaningful way. While research does suggest that the use of signing can enhance children's overall communication skills, this may not be the case for every child. The activities and information in this book are in no way intended to substitute for the expertise and assistance of a speech-language pathologist, and are not meant to replace speech or language therapy. If you have any concerns about the development of your child, particularly in the area of communication, please talk to your pediatrician or contact your local school district for screening information.

Tabitha signs WHAT?

HAND FORMATIONS

The adult models in pictures throughout the book demonstrate the vocabulary using American Sign Language (ASL). Here are some key hand formations that you will use in basic sign vocabulary. Hand formation references appear in italics.

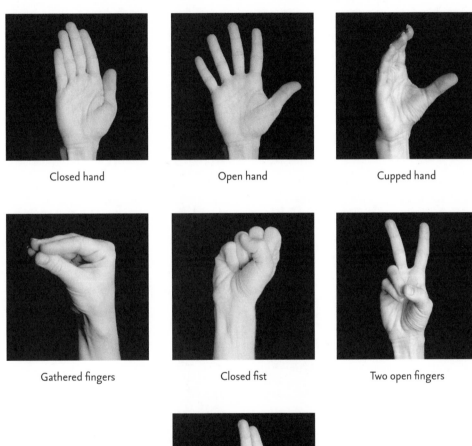

Closed hand   Open hand   Cupped hand

Gathered fingers   Closed fist   Two open fingers

Two closed fingers

Note that teaching finger spelling and extensive ASL vocabulary is beyond the scope of this book. If you are interested in learning ASL in more depth, there are courses that may be available to you in your community that teach the grammar, syntax, and vocabulary unique to American Sign Language, which is utilized in communication with most deaf adults. In addition, Michigan State University has developed a Web site called the American Sign Language Vocabulary Browser (http://commtechlab.msu.edu/sites/aslweb/browser.htm) that provides short video clips of thousands of signs. Many parents find this or other similar sign language video dictionaries on the Web to be helpful in learning new signs to teach their child that have meaning and importance for their whole family.

Keaton signs BEAR.

SIGNING WITH BOOKS

It is never too early to teach children a love for books. Just as music communicates deep feelings and ideas in a manner that words cannot, books have a unique power to engage the mind and the imagination. Perhaps one of the reasons that babies love books is that it gives them something to both see and hear—they can listen to their favorite voices reading the words as they look at the colorful and interesting pages. Over time, the pictures become recognizable to children as representations of important objects and experiences in their world. They love to pause to point to things they recognize when asked questions like "Where is the picture of the COW on this page? Can you touch the picture of the COOKIE on that page?"

With lots of repetition, the child begins to anticipate the events in the story and develops the ability to predict what happens next. His attention moves from identifying items pictured to wanting to turn the page to make sure that the page with the boy playing music will be followed by the page with the dog barking a tune. He will also start to look at the pictures on the page from left to right just as he will someday do when it is time to read words.

A child's ability to point to pictures that have meaning for him, to anticipate events in a story, and to follow the story from the left-hand side of the page to the right are all important skills for future reading success. Reading books also supports the goal of sign language learning, as this special time between you and your child affords you a wonderful opportunity to sign as you read. This is typically a time when your little one is quiet and focused on you and the book you are prepared to share. Place the child on your lap facing out, set the book in your lap, and use your hands in front of his body to sign key vocabulary words you find in the text.

To enhance the sign language learning during reading time, make sure you choose books that have rhyme and repetition. You can always repeat the signed words on the page for extra practice. Be creative in including sign vocabulary by changing a word or two in the text to include more of the signs you wish to teach. You will be able to get away with this for a few more years until he starts to memorize the text and scolds you for reading it "wrong."

Take care not to overwhelm your child with sign language to avoid spoiling the closeness and security he feels with you as you snuggle and read. Add signs gradually as you read books to him. Repetition is necessary for learning the books as well as for understanding and using sign language.

One of the unique benefits of singing and signing with toddlers is that the music provides a meaningful and enjoyable context for repeating and practicing the sign vocabulary. Book reading accomplishes the same goal. With lots of repetition, your child will learn to turn the pages of his favorite book and sign the words you have practiced together.

● ● ● ● ● ● ● ●

THE BENEFITS OF
TODDLER SING & SIGN
FREQUENTLY ASKED QUESTIONS

To **HELP YOU** better understand the nature and benefits of *Toddler Sing & Sign,* I have solicited the opinions of some wise and experienced parents and caregivers who have used the program. Here is their practical advice to some of the most commonly asked questions and answers.

Q: What is *Toddler Sing & Sign*?

> *Toddler Sing & Sign* is a fun collection of songs, signs, activities, and picture book suggestions. It helped us to be able to sign new concepts and ideas our daughter was beginning to understand but couldn't yet express with spoken words. She loves the animals and colors theme, and insists on singing and dancing to her special songs every day. She loves to sign "rooster" as she dances around our kitchen. She stomps her feet to her "grizzly bear" beat. This book helped us support her as she began to transition from signing to speaking. It also really helped us bond with her by giving us fun things to do together as a family.
>
> —WENDY J.

Toddler Sing & Sign is a fun, interactive technique used to engage your child in meaningful communication. Toddlers' vocabulary is still limited and their frustration threshold is reached quickly. *Toddler Sing & Sign* provides a continuing base for fundamental language needs. It sets the stage for sound learning in reading, oral communication and success.

—JONANN E.

Toddler Sing & Sign creates a wonderful opportunity for parent and child to interact and communicate through music and gesture.

—MARY J.

Q: How does *Toddler Sing & Sign* differ from *Baby Sing & Sign*?

Toddler Sing & Sign is a spunkier version of *Baby Sing & Sign,* with upbeat songs and signs perfectly suited for our busy boy—and lots of the motor activities he loves. There are also many other developmental benefits included that we appreciate, such as prereading skills and experiences that begin to prepare him for preschool.

—KEVIN R.

I loved the *Baby Sing & Sign* program for my infant, and we had a blast using the games and tunes to teach my daughter to sign during the first year and a half of her life. Now that she is walking and trying to talk, we were thrilled to have a new program that had music and activities uniquely geared to the interests of an active two-year-old. She loves animals and colors, and the songs are great for dancing and singing!

—SARAH B.

Q: Will my toddler still learn to speak if I teach her to sign?

Your child will speak when he or she is good and ready. My daughter did not even say "Mama" or "Dada" until 16 or so months, yet she would sign them along with many others. When I would put her to sleep at night she would be signing "doggie" or some other wonderful thing she had thought of about her day, and I knew she was telling me things without saying a word. It is very precious.

—MARYLEE L.

Yes! Teaching sign to your toddler will not only help him/her communicate with you better, but it will also increase his/her vocabulary. I found that once I taught my daughter to sign a word, it very quickly became a part of her signing AND speaking vocabulary. In time, she stopped signing and spoke the word instead.

—MYRA V.

Q: Why should I use sign language with my hearing toddler?

Because of all the wonderful things you will learn about them and communicate with them before they speak. They can also express thoughts and ideas because they can sign words they cannot say. You will be amazed at how much your child knows and thinks, because the sign language provides a "window" for you to gaze inside their minds and know what they are thinking and feeling!

—BRIAN L.

Sign language is a very effective tool in communicating with toddlers. Since the signs are concrete, the toddler can visualize their wants and communicate through signing. Often, toddlers may have trouble expressing themselves through talking, so signing is a good alternative.

—ALAN L.

Q: Is baby sign language a fad?

Baby sign language is more than a fad; it's a means to an end! My child easily transitioned to words based on the success she had communicating her needs. We are learning so much about how the human brain works, baby sign language is just the beginning for what lies ahead. The future is about tapping into endless possibilities; why not begin with age-appropriate language?

—KAREN T.

I don't think anything as beneficial as baby sign can be fad. To me it is like asking if disposable diapers and baby wipes are a fad.

—Ruth D.

Q: My toddler is very active and always on the go. How will I ever be able to teach him any signs if I can't get him to sit still long enough to watch me complete a sign?

Children do not have to be sitting still to learn from their parents. If parents models consistent signs while they speak, the child will pick them up. Our children mimic everything we do; just be patient as they practice and learn. Remember, repetition, repetition, repetition. Make it a constant, make it fun and "they will come!"

—Sara P.

Did you teach your toddler to put a phone to his ear or push the buttons on a remote? Probably not! It is like when a baby wants your keys to play with: they watch EVERYTHING you do and you don't even realize it. If you just start using sign without "trying to teach" it, they will eventually start to imitate you and do it in their own way.

—GRETA R.

Q: My toddler can't make the sign exactly right, and it doesn't even look like the child in the pictures.

Sometimes, toddlers make adaptations of the real sign. The important thing is that you, the parent, understand what he/she is trying to say. As fine-motor skills develop, the sign your toddler makes may start to look more like the sign in the pictures.

—ALICE A.

The sign probably won't be perfect and will be done as the child can. Some children will even make up their own signs based on their abilities and perception. It is important that parent and child understand what the sign is so that effective communication can occur.

—ANGELA W.

In my personal experience, very few infants and toddlers sign exactly the same. We met a little girl who approached us at a function and starting signing "more" in textbook fashion as my little girl was eating a muffin. I obviously knew she wanted some to eat. However, if my daughter had signed her version of "more" to this child's mother, she might have interpreted her sign as "hurt." That's just the way my child's sign looks. As her parent I know her and what she is trying to communicate because I am with her all of the time. Similarly, when she was an infant, I recognized that her "hungry cry" was different from her "tired cry." Other people couldn't hear the difference. The key is to know your child and treat their signed communication as language from the start. With age and practice, their signing may become more exact.

—STEPHANIE L.

Q: I sign while I speak to my toddler and I see that she understands me. She says a few words and can imitate some words, but she only uses a couple of signs occasionally. Should I be concerned that she isn't signing very much?

Signing is all about repetition. It is okay if she only signs a couple of words at first. The more she sees it, the more she will start to make the association and it will have some meaning for her.

—DAN P.

Q: My child can talk. Why would I want to teach her to sign?

Abstract concepts, like feelings, can be difficult for young children to understand and verbalize. Signing is one way to show the abstract concept—such as "hurt" or "happy"—in a concrete way. This helps to give real meaning to the words they hear and say.

—ELADIO V.

While toddlers are beginning to communicate through speech, they may get frustrated or not be able to say the word they want to. Sometimes, when our three-year-old daughter is tired or sick, she may use signs to communicate because she doesn't have the energy to speak. By having our children use sign language as a supplement to spoken language, we have avoided frustration, because they are better able to communicate with us.

—GWEN L.

Q: My toddler is just entering the "terrible twos" and is beginning to have tantrums. Could sign language help?

As a parent of a two-year-old boy I have found signing to be a very effective way to reduce the number of tantrums we see in our home. Tantrums are typically the result of a child not being able to effectively communicate their frustrations and/or needs to their caregiver. Therefore, the sign that has worked to help stop tantrums before they start is the sign for "help." Although Gianni is now able to say the word, he will still do the sign while saying "help" if he is truly frustrated. I'm able to quickly offer assistance while connecting the verbal reason for his frustration before he loses control. As a parent educator I have introduced this sign to families of infants and toddlers as another strategy to aid in taming a tantrum.

—AMY S.

Q: We taught our baby to sign, and my three-year-old still signs *please* and *more* among other signs when he speaks. Is this okay? When will he stop this?

It is absolutely fine. Although he will likely stop signing once he learns to speak, he will probably remember the signs. I taught my son sign language as an infant, but stopped using it with him around two years of age. When we started using it again for my younger son, he started back up again. I see it as a huge positive! Not only is he reinforcing the sign language learning for his brother, but my sons are able to communicate with one another in their own special language.

—MARY ANNE H.

When our three-year-old son wants to be very sure we understand him, he'll sign as he says what he wants. This most often happens when he wants to do something again. He'll sign "more" while saying "again, again, again." The signing is every bit as clear as his words are. Now that we are introducing signs to his seven-month-old baby brother, he follows along with us. He remembers all of the signs that were once the primary method of communication for him when he was a baby. Our three-year-old has fun helping us teach them to his baby brother. Our three-year-old likes to tease us using signs. He'll sign "monkey" and say something else. Then he'll giggle. He knows he is saying one thing and signing another. He's turned it into a game.

—HEATHER G.

Q: My two-year-old is using many signs we taught him to communicate with us. However, he isn't talking very much. Should I be worried?

Many people think if a child signs, he won't use their words. This is just as ungrounded as the belief that children have to crawl before they walk! Is your child communicating his needs? Is your child understanding what you say to him by following simple directions and responding to your spoken words? Children who are kinesthetic learners learn best by touching and doing than by looking or listening, and may initially prefer signing to speech. Make sure you continue to use words with the signs to ensure that he makes a verbal and physical connection to the language.

—KEN R.

If you have a concern about your child's hearing or speech, then I would consult your child's pediatrician, but I would not be worried that it has anything to do with the signs he is utilizing.

—FRANK M.

Q: I've listened to the CD, and my child can't remember all of the words or sing fast enough to sing along. Is it okay to just dance and enjoy the music sometimes?

Yes! Children love music and love to dance. You can use any opportunity to listen and move to music with your child. It's not only great exercise, but it's also just a lot of fun!

—OLIVIA C.

I think dancing and enjoying the CD is the primary reason to listen to the music. The recorded music is an aid to me in learning the signs, because it provides the repetition my child and I need to master this new language skill.

—BETH S.

The wonder of music is that all people from infants to grandparents can enjoy music at their own pace. There are so many aspects of the music for young children to attend to: rhythm, instruments, lyrics, singers, and all the extra tone colors that make the song a story in and of itself. Music is the universal language, and a perfect complement to performing sign language for expression and joy!

—ANGELA W.

GETTING STARTED

As you begin signing with your child, keep these tips in mind:

○ Teach one sign at a time until you have shared up to five or six signs with your toddler. Be consistent in saying and signing the words often. When your child begins to use any of these signs to communicate with you, you can begin to add new signs to your child's vocabulary.

○ Always speak as well as sign the word. You are teaching your child to respond to both your verbal and signed communication.

○ You may use either hand to form the signs.

○ Use facial expressions that reinforce what you are trying to communicate.

○ Give your toddler adequate time to respond before repeating signs.

○ Continue to sign to your child even if she does not sign to you. Although you may not see your child forming signs and using them to communicate with you, she most likely understands the words and signs you use to communicate with her.

○ Look for an *approximation,* or "best try," as your child attempts to imitate the signs you teach.

○ Be positive and encouraging. Don't forget to have fun!

Maizie signs HIPPO.

SECRETS OF SUCCESS WITH SINGING AND SIGNING

○ Let your child direct you in selecting signs that have importance for him. Your child may have an affinity for COWS or may adore the color YELLOW. Start with what he cares about most.

○ Make your sign teaching a natural part of your day. Language learning requires a meaningful context.

○ Take "baby steps" in incorporating the ideas from this book into your child's life. Play with a sign and a song for as long as it takes for both of you to feel confident you have mastered the material.

○ You will undoubtedly tire of the songs and activities long before your child. But the goal of *Toddler Sing & Sign* is to support your child's emerging speech—as well as his interest in playful exploration, books, and love for learning. This requires opportunities to practice. Remember: *Repetition is good. Repetition is good. Repetition is good.*

○ Remind yourself often that the real reason for doing sign language and music with your child is to have fun!

Avery signs EAT.

1

ALL AROUND THE KITCHEN

ANIMAL WORDS TO LEARN: **ROOSTER, BEAR, FISH**
COLOR WORD TO LEARN: **RED**
OTHER WORDS TO LEARN: **STOP, BIG, MUSIC/SONG**
*BONUS WORDS TO LEARN: **MOMMY*, DADDY*, DANCE*,
JUMP*, RUN*, WALK/STRUT*, SIT/CHAIR*, HAIR*, TOE*, LITTLE***

The original version of this song is believed to have been created by schoolgirls in Alabama in the 1930s and is wonderful for movement play. Perhaps they jumped rope on the playground or at the park as they sang.

Chorus:

All around the kitchen,	*Dance in place,*
Cock-a-doodle-doodle-doo,	*sign ROOSTER*
All around the kitchen,	*Dance in place,*
Cock-a-doodle-doodle-doo,	*sign ROOSTER*
All around the kitchen,	*Dance in place,*
Cock-a-doodle-doodle-doo,	*sign ROOSTER*
All around the kitchen,	*Dance in place,*
Cock-a-doodle-doodle-doo,	*sign ROOSTER*

Verse 1:

Well, you STOP like this,	*Sign STOP and freeze!*
Cock-a-doodle-doodle-doo,	
Then you STRUT your feet,	*Walk in place*
Cock-a-doodle-doodle-doo,	
To the ROOSTER beat,	*Sign ROOSTER and walk in place*
Cock-a-doodle-doodle-doo,	

---

* These bonus signs are found in the *Toddler Sing & Sign* Dictionary (page 207).

STRUT around in a circle, Cock-a-doodle-doodle-doo,	*Walk in circle*
Verse 2:	
Well, you STOP like this, Cock-a-doodle-doodle-doo,	*Sign STOP and freeze!*
Put your paws in the air, Cock-a-doodle-doodle-doo,	*Lift arms in the air or sign* BIG
Like a BIG ol' BEAR, Cock-a-doodle-doodle-doo,	*Sign BEAR*
Then you shake your HAIR, Cock-a-doodle-doodle-doo,	*Shake your hair from side to side*
Verse 3:	
Well, you STOP like this, Cock-a-doodle-doodle-doo,	*Sign STOP and freeze!*
Now you swim like a FISH, Cock-a-doodle-doodle-doo,	*Sign FISH*
Swim fast if you wish, Cock-a-doodle-doodle-doo,	*Sign FISH*
You go splish-splash-splish, Cock-a-doodle-doodle-doo,	*Sign FISH*
Verse 4:	
Well, you STOP like this, Cock-a-doodle-doodle-doo,	*Sign STOP and freeze!*
Now you DANCE down low, Cock-a-doodle-doodle-doo,	*Bend knees and dance lower*
How low can you go? Cock-a-doodle-doodle-doo,	*Dance and move still lower*
Can you touch your TOE, whoa, whoa, whoa, whoa?	Touch your toes; *then stand*

Verse 5:

Now, there's a ROOSTER in the kitchen,	*Sign ROOSTER*
We're all RUNNING in the kitchen,	*Run in place*
My DADDY's JUMPING in the kitchen,	*Jump up and down*
My MOMMA boogies in the kitchen . . .	*Dance in place*

Coda:

All around the kitchen,	*Dance in place*
All around that kitchen	*Dance in place*
We're making MUSIC in the kitchen	*Sign MUSIC*
There's a ROOSTER in the kitchen	*Sign ROOSTER*
All around the kitchen	*Dance in place*
My MOMMA BOOGIES in the kitchen	*Dance in place*
There's a FISHIE in the kitchen	*Sign FISH*
Boogity-boogity-boogity kitchen,	*Dance in place*
All around the kitchen	*Dance in place*
There's a BEAR in the kitchen	*Sign BEAR*
He's in my CHAIR in the kitchen!	*Sign BEAR*
All around the kitchen,	*Dance in place*
DADDY's JUMPING in the kitchen	*Jump in place*
There's a ROOSTER in the kitchen	*Sign ROOSTER*
I'm gonna BOOGIE in the kitchen	*Dance in place*
Dooo . . .	*Sign MUSIC*

ALL AROUND THE KITCHEN

Traditional / Adapted by Anne Meeker Miller

 **ROOSTER**

Make a rooster's "comb" with thumb, curved pointer and middle fingers, and tap forehead.

Child may place her thumb or hand on her cheek, brow, or other head location.

 **BEAR**

Cross hands on body and scratch, showing a "bear hug."

Child may scratch shoulders or tummy without crossing her arms.

 **FISH**

Hold one *closed hand,* thumb side up, with other *closed hand* touching at wrist. Move both hands forward, with front hand fluttering to imitate fish swimming.

Child may use one hand fluttering forward to imitate a swimming fish, or grasp one hand on other arm or wrist.

RED

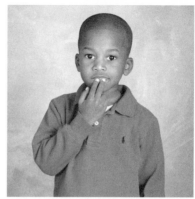

Pointer finger moves down across the lips, showing their red color.

Child may touch his lips with all fingers or may simply pucker his lips.

STOP

Move little-finger side of one *closed hand* abruptly onto palm of other hand in a single chopping motion.

Child may clap one hand to another or place *closed hands* in front of her body.

BIG

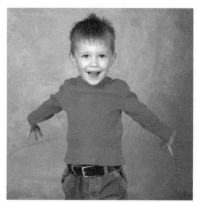

Closed hands with thumb against palm face each other and pull apart to show their large size.

Child may skip the hands-together motion and hold his arms wide or over head.

MUSIC

Wave the palm of one *closed hand* over the other extended arm. Sweep hand back and forth from wrist to shoulder.

Child may wave one or both arms at her sides.

TIPS FOR INTRODUCING
ALL AROUND THE KITCHEN

○ Start your sign teaching with the words ROOSTER and STOP. Perform the ROOSTER sign each time you sing the lyric: "Cock-a-doodle-doodle-doo." Sign STOP and hold very still as you sing: "Well, you STOP like this. . . ." The rest of the song can be an opportunity to dance or you can walk in a circle as you sing.

○ Add BEAR and FISH signs after your child has enjoyed signing ROOSTER and STOP during the song.

○ The sign language directions for each song include signed words I would reasonably expect a toddler to be able to do as they listen to the music. Where there are several signed word choices in a phrase, parents should pick just one word until the toddler has been singing and signing the song for awhile. With repetition and time, they will be able to sign two-word combinations. Judging by how much the toddlers I know love the songs, there will be ample opportunities for repetition and practice.

○ In the fifth verse, the song lyrics describe "mama boogies" and "daddy jumping" in the kitchen. Your toddler may want to sign the words MOMMY and DADDY. However, most toddlers would prefer doing the "jump" and "dance" actions instead. Likewise, most toddlers enjoy actually running and jumping rather than performing the signs for RUN and JUMP. We considered these toddler preferences in devising sign language directions for the songs.

♪ More Musical Fun with *All Around the Kitchen*

● The final section of the song is wonderful for focused listening. I like to stop singing after the "touch your toe—whoa-whoa . . ." section and simply listen and sign the animals and actions. I use facial expression to let the toddler know I am concentrating on listening to the music. Say key words such as the animal names as you sign them during the final narrative of the recording.

● "All Around the Kitchen" is the perfect song for adding a kitchen band complete with plastic or metal mixing bowls, bread or cake pans, and pots. Use utensils such as wooden or plastic spoons or spatulas for "drumsticks." *Always remain close to your toddler to monitor her safety.* Have your child move her hands to shorten the length of the wooden spoon or spatula used to play. This will prevent your toddler from inadvertently hitting herself. Tell her you love her kitchen music.

- Two-year-old Emery likes to walk in a circle around her living room (or kitchen!) as she enjoys "All Around the Kitchen." She then stops walking when she hears the word "STOP." She also signs ROOSTER and says "cock-a-doodle-doo." When the song is over, she will walk to her daddy and tell him "cock-a-doodle-doo" with an expectant look on her face. This means, "I want more of the 'All Around the Kitchen' song." They then begin the singing and signing all over again.

- Eighteen-month-old Tabitha isn't using any spoken words to express herself yet, but she can sing the "whoa, whoa, whoa, whoa!" lyric to perfection! Encourage your child to imitate your vocal sounds. Play with sounds that animals make, say a series of words that rhyme with your child's name, or start with one consonant sound and create a silly string of syllables. Your rhyme and sound play doesn't have to incorporate real words. The purpose of sound play with toddlers is to help them figure out how to coordinate their breath, lips, and tongue to produce the same sounds they hear you make.

Children learn to imitate vocal sounds by watching and listening to you.

GAMES AND ACTIVITIES

♪ Sensory Kitchen

VOCABULARY PRACTICE: ROOSTER, BEAR, STOP, MUSIC, WALK*, DANCE*, JUMP*, RUN*

DEVELOPMENTAL BENEFITS: sensory exploration, tactile stimulation, balance, fine- and gross-motor movements

MATERIALS: plastic bin or tub, rice, cornmeal, or other dried food items, such as flour, dry oatmeal, and Malt-O-Meal, pictures of animals or animal toys, large blanket or plastic tablecloth, small animal toys or pictures

Rice bin play promotes tactile stimulation—a heightened sensory experience of touch.

DIRECTIONS: Place a plastic bin on a large blanket or tablecloth, and fill the bin with rice or cornmeal. Place one to two inches of rice or cornmeal in the bottom of the tub.

To begin, allow your child to touch and feel the cornmeal. Sing as you listen to the "All Around the Kitchen" music, and show your child how to draw a circle in the cornmeal each time you hear the lyric "all around the kitchen." With practice, your child may be able to draw in the cornmeal all on her own as she hears the "kitchen" music phrase.

Once your child is comfortable with the *tactile stimulation,* or how it feels to touch the cornmeal with her fingertips, invite her to take off her shoes and socks and stand in the plastic tub. Be sure to hold her hand while she is standing in the tub. If your child is hesitant to do so, show her how to do it.

Play the "All Around the Kitchen" song, and listen for action words—such as WALK, DANCE, JUMP, or RUN—as they occur in the song. When you hear an action word, perform the *gross-motor* movement with your feet still in the cornmeal bin. Sign STOP as well as the action words while you do your fancy "kitchen dance." Allow your child to sit in the cornmeal as well!

For safety purposes during this activity, sign the words before and after the action so that

---

*   These bonus signs are found in the *Toddler Sing & Sign* Dictionary (page 207).

your hands are free to assist your child while she is in motion. Be a vigilant "spotter" during this activity, ready to catch or stabilize your child as her feet move within the bin.

You can add measuring cups, funnels, or utensils such as whisks or spoons to your cornmeal bin. Your child may want to mix and pour the materials, or perhaps make you an imaginary "snack" in her Sensory Kitchen. This gives your toddler a chance to practice her *fine motor* movements, or motions performed with her fingers and hands. You may also want to add small animal pictures or toys to cue your child to the animal you are imitating, such as BEAR or ROOSTER.

Some children are sensitive to touch and hesitant to try new things. The key with all sensory activities is to involve your child in the games gradually. If she does not want to touch the cornmeal or stand in the tub, do not pressure her to do so. Invite her again the next time you are playing Sensory Kitchen. She will join in when she is ready.

♪ Rooster Hat

VOCABULARY PRACTICE: **ROOSTER, RED, MUSIC, STOP, WALK/ STRUT*, DANCE*, JUMP*, RUN***

DEVELOPMENTAL BENEFITS: creative and imaginative play, gross-motor movements

MATERIALS: ball cap (preferably white or black), red glove, pillow filling (or other stuffing material, such as tissue paper or facial tissues), needle and thread

Isaac is amused and enthralled with his mother's Rooster Hat.

DIRECTIONS: Create a Rooster Hat so that your child can "be" the rooster. Stuff the glove with pillow filling and stitch the glove closed. Next, stitch the base of the glove to the bill of the ball cap and the tip of the thumb to the front of the cap.

Children make sense of their life experiences through dramatic play opportunities. Place the Rooster Hat on your child and watch her "become" a rooster. Turn on the rooster music and have fun moving and dancing to "All Around the Kitchen." Make a Rooster Hat for yourself and join in the fun. WALK, DANCE, JUMP,

---

* These bonus signs are found in the *Toddler Sing & Sign* Dictionary (page 207).

RUN, and STOP to the music. Say or sing and sign each action as you perform it. Experience the music through your child's movements and signs and have fun while you STRUT your new "rooster-do."

♪ Reading "RED-iness" Book

VOCABULARY PRACTICE: RED

DEVELOPMENTAL BENEFITS: classifying objects by color, book engagement, vocabulary building

MATERIALS: small photo album OR four sheets of 8½ x11–inch black or white construction paper cut in half, stapler, masking or plastic tape, magazines or digital camera and printer

Reading "RED-iness" Book

DIRECTIONS: Cut paper in half and staple left side to make a Reading "RED-iness" Book. Cover the stapled edge of the book with colored masking or plastic tape. You can also use a small photo album for your red book and paste a red label on the cover. Many photo centers give out free small photo albums to customers with the purchase of prints.

Take a walk through your house and help your child find objects from her daily experiences that are red. Then take digital photographs of these items, print the pictures, and paste them into the book. Find something that is not red and add that photograph to the last page of the book. As an alternative, you could find pictures of red things in a magazine and cut them out. Then allow your child to pick four or five of these pictures that have meaning for her. They could then be glued into the pages of your red book.

"Read" the book together, repeating for each page the sentence: "The ____ ____ is RED." Fill in the blank with the word pictured on each page. Sign RED as you read each page, as well as the names of the objects pictured if you know their signs. On the final page, say, "The _____ is *not* RED." You and your child can play this Reading "RED-iness" Book game together and make new books for other colors.

A SIGN OF SUCCESS

♪ HURRY UP AND WAIT: CELEBRATING YOUR ♪ TODDLER'S "TERRIBLE TWOS"

I believe it was about ten minutes ago that I gave birth to our first son. He decided to arrive slightly ahead of schedule and caught us off guard. I didn't own a diaper, Onesie, baby bottle, or mommy bathrobe appropriate to wear during hospital visiting hours. As is his fashion, he arrived on his terms exactly seven weeks before my due date.

I remember the first time my husband and I ventured out of our house with our new son in tow. Off we went with Andy in his little infant seat, tiny and jaundiced, looking roughly the size of an elongated cantaloupe. I loaded our important purchases—one each of the pacifiers commercially available in the baby aisle of Wal-Mart, nursing pads, Epsom salts, and Mint Milano cookies—around Andy's infant seat, parked inconveniently in the middle of the grocery cart. And I recall saying a little prayer, asking for my son to soon be big and strong enough to ride on my hip with casual ease as I strolled through my new life as a mom.

Without much exaggeration, I must tell you that in the ten minutes that have passed since that little heart-to-heart I had with God, Andy has grown into a young man with a driver's permit and a keen interest in blonde cheerleaders. If it weren't for my little Mint Milano habit, he could likely carry *me* through the Wal-Mart on his hip.

As parents we often become entangled in the contradictions of our own thoughts. We want our babies to be small and snuggly and smell vaguely of peach baby food and Johnson's baby shampoo forever. Yet we frequently find ourselves saying silently to ourselves (and sometimes out loud) things like "I can't wait until little Sophie can walk so her clothes stay cleaner," or "Won't it be grand when Manuel can speak in complete sentences so we won't have to worry about his language development any longer?" I'm convinced that this tug-of-war game we play with ourselves as parents—the urge to hold on to our children too tightly in the same instant we wish we could set them free—must be universal. I have never met a parent who didn't shake his or her head vigorously in agreement when I share this guilty secret.

DOG is certain to be a word your toddler will sign if you own one.

I mention this notion to you because I think it is likely that you know and love a toddler. By "toddler" I mean in the classic sense "one who toddles" or travels on his own two feet, however tentatively. Once a child begins to walk, she is issued her Toddler Club membership card and hangs with this crowd until she is of legal age to attend preschool.

Toddlers as a group have, as they say nowadays, some "issues." Often called the Terrible Twos, these wee folk have gotten a lot of bad press. It is true that as a group they are often violently frustrated. They like to think they have all of their personal choices under control and don't need much adult interference. Their moods swing wildly from bubbly/happy to outraged/unreasonable. Their frustration is compounded by the fact that no one seems to understand their speech, when they have a fervent need to express their ideas and desires. They are also incapable of sharing their stuff with others. (The only exception to the latter being the family dog, who routinely ends up having hotdog bites and cheese cubes dropped on his head. However, if the truth be told, toddlers aren't technically *sharing* with Fido. They just want to see which food groups bounce.)

> Toddler frustration is compounded by the fact that no one seems to understand their speech, when they have a fervent need to express their ideas and desires.

The good news is that all of that quirky toddler behavior is purposeful and necessary as they begin their journey toward independence. They are especially proud of their newfound freedom to move about, and they spend most of their free time working on their walking and running proficiency—as well as their ability to get into trouble. But no two toddlers are alike. There are great differences between children when it comes to the rate at which they learn to walk, talk, solve problems, and get along with others.

As luck would have it, after months of repetition, playful interactions, and exuberant family "sing-and-sign-alongs," your child may finally be using the signs you so patiently taught her using the *Toddler Sing & Sign* program at the exact moment she joins her comrades in The Toddlerhood. As your toddler becomes increasingly more mobile, face-to-face sign language teaching that requires sitting and gazing at each other becomes less desirable to her. She is far too busy perfecting her large-motor and problem-solving skills to pause for long enough to figure out what you are doing so urgently with your hands and voice.

As your child's first and best teacher, you may experience some frustration of your own while earnestly trying to teach signed words to a creature who more closely resembles

Wile E. Coyote than the docile, stop-and-smell-the-Cheerios baby you held in your arms only a few weeks ago.

Hurry up and wait. It's that thing we do when we wish a day or a season of our lives away in anticipation of what comes next, certain it will be a vast improvement on the challenges of parenting today. So while you're waiting, join your rascally little toddler in a game of "Toss the Cereal to Fido" in the backyard. And memorize forever the image of that little girl who is signing CEREAL with sticky hands and a devilish grin.

BOOKS TO READ

Toddlers and animals come in all sizes. P. D. Eastman, protégé of Dr. Seuss and the talented author of numerous children's books, introduces us to two happy-go-lucky pups who are friends despite their obvious differences. One likes green paint while the other prefers red; one likes to ski while the other likes to skate; and as your child will observe in Eastman's amusing illustrations, one dog is big and one is little. In *Big Dog . . . Little Dog* (Random House), the doggie friends have a fine adventure and solve some very big problems.

Eastman's dog tale reminds readers large and small that our differences can unite us rather than divide us. Big lessons can be contained in little stories.

ROOSTER

Cock-A-Doodle Dudley by Bill Peet (Scholastic)

Cook-A-Doodle-Doo! by Janet Stevens and Susan Stevens Crummel (Voyager Books)

Rooster's Off to See the World by Eric Carle (Aladdin)

The Bossy Rooster by Margaret Nash (Picture Window Books)

Who Wakes Rooster? by Clare Hodgson Meeker (Simon & Schuster Children's Publishing)

BEAR

Bear Wants More by Karma Wilson (Margaret K. McElderry)

Bear's Day by Lisa Campbell Ernst (Viking Juvenile)

Don't Wake Up the Bear by Marjorie Dennis Murray (Marshall Cavendish Children's Books)

Jamberry by Bruce Degen (HarperCollins)

Sleepy Bears by Mem Fox (Harcourt Children's Books)

FISH

Fidgety Fish by Ruth Galloway (Tiger Tales)

Fish Eyes: A Book You Can Count On by Lois Ehlert (Voyager Books)

Friendly Fish by Wendy McLean (Book Company Publishing)

Hooray for Fish by Lucy Cousins (Candlewick Press)

Ten Little Fish by Audrey and Bruce Wood (Blue Sky Press)

RED

Big Red Barn by Margaret Wise Brown (HarperCollins)

Gossie by Olivier Dunrea (Houghton Mifflin)

Peek-a-Who? A Lift-the-Flap Book by Moira Butterfield (Cartwheel Books)

Put Me in the Zoo: A Book of Colors by Robert Lopshire (Random House)

Red Fish, Blue Fish, Old Fish, New Fish: An Utterly Stupendous Vinyl Extravaganza! Bath Book by Dr. Seuss (Random House Books for Young Readers)

WALK

A Good Night Walk by Elisha Cooper (Orchard Books)

Autumn Walk by Ann Burg (HarperFestival)

I Went Walking by Sue Williams (Red Wagon Books)

Spot's First Walk by Eric Hill (Putnam Juvenile)

Walk On! A Guide for Babies of All Ages by Marla Frazee (Harcourt Children's Books)

STOP

Bus Stops by Taro Gomi (Chronicle Books)

Next Stop by Sarah Ellis (Fitzhenry and Whiteside)

Red, Stop! Green, Go! by P. D. Eastman (Random House Books for Young Readers)

Stop, Train, Stop! A Thomas the Tank Engine Story by W. Rev Awdry (Random House Books for Young Readers)

The Tale of Peter Rabbit by Beatrix Potter (F. Warne)

BIG

Big and Little by Samantha Berger and Pamela Chanko (Scholastic)

Big Like Me by Anna Grossnickle Hines (Greenwillow Books)

Big Little by Leslie Patricelli (Candlewick Press)

How Big Is a Pig? by Clare Beaton (Barefoot Books)

Little Bear Is a Big Brother by Jutta Langreuter and Vera Sobat (Millbrook Press)

MUSIC

Animal Music by Harriet Ziefert (Houghton Mifflin)

Baby Danced the Polka by Karen Beaumont (Dial Books for Young Readers)

Clap Your Hands by Lorinda Bryan Cauley (Putnam Juvenile)

Pots and Pans by Patricia Hubbell (HarperCollins)

We All Sing with the Same Voice by J. Philip Miller (HarperFestival)

2

GRIZZLY BEAR

COLOR SIGNS TO LEARN: **BROWN**
OTHER SIGNS TO LEARN: **LOOK/SEE, SCARED/AFRAID**
WORDS TO REVIEW: **BEAR, BIG, MOMMY*, DADDY*, HAIR***
BONUS SIGN: **EYES***

This Southern ballad tells the tale of a big brown bear and brave Daddy's search for the wily critter. Children can help tell the story by singing the repeated "Grizzly Bear" phrase as they stomp their "paws" to the beat.

Verse 1:
I'm gonna tell y'a little story
'bout a grizzly BEAR;   *Sign BEAR*
Tell y'a little story
'bout a grizzly BEAR.   *Sign BEAR*
Well, a great BIG grizzly,   *Sign BIG*
grizzly BEAR;   *Sign BEAR*
A great BIG grizzly,   *Sign BIG*
grizzly BEAR.   *Sign BEAR*

Chorus:
Grizzly, grizzly, grizzly BEAR   *Sign BEAR*
Grizzly, grizzly, grizzly BEAR . . .   *Sign BEAR*

Verse 2:
Well, my MOMMA was a-SCARED   *Sign SCARED or MOMMA SCARED*
of that grizzly BEAR;   *Sign BEAR*

---

* These bonus signs are found in the *Toddler Sing & Sign* Dictionary (page 207).

My MOMMA was a-SCARED	*Sign SCARED*
of that grizzly BEAR.	*Sign BEAR*
So my DADDY went a-LOOKIN'	*Sign LOOK or DADDY LOOK*
for that grizzly BEAR;	*Sign BEAR*
My DADDY went a-LOOKIN'	*Sign LOOK or DADDY LOOK*
for that grizzly BEAR.	*Sign BEAR*

Verse 3:

He had long, long HAIR,	*Touch hair or sign HAIR*
That grizzly BEAR;	*Sign BEAR*
He had long, long HAIR,	*Touch hair or sign HAIR*
that grizzly BEAR.	*Sign BEAR*
He had big blue EYES,	*Touch eyes or sign EYES*
that grizzly BEAR;	*Sign BEAR*
He had big blue EYES,	*Touch eyes or sign EYES*
that grizzly BEAR.	*Sign BEAR*

GRIZZLY BEAR

Traditional / Adapted by Anne Meeker Miller

BROWN

Pull *closed hand* with thumb against palm down along side of face.

Child may touch or tap cheek with fingertips.

LOOK/SEE

Place tips of *two open fingers* under eyes and swing out as if to "look" at something.

Child may point to eyes or the object he "sees," or perform the sign with both hands.

SCARED/ AFRAID

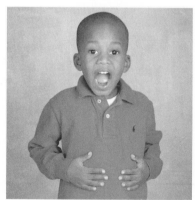

Open hands with palm facing body move toward and away from each other with "scared" facial expression.

Child may place hands on tummy and change his facial expression.

TIPS FOR INTRODUCING
GRIZZLY BEAR

○ Start simply by signing BEAR as you sing the word during each verse. Then walk to the beat on the repeating chorus: "Grizzly, grizzly, grizzly BEAR!"

○ When you sing, "My MOMMA was a-SCARED of that grizzly BEAR," be sure to show your child your most expressive scared face with your eyebrows raised and your eyes wide. Ask your child to show you his scared face. Praise him for any facial expression he shares.

○ If you like, you can walk to the beat of the repeating chorus: "Grizzly, grizzly, grizzly BEAR!" Walking in place to a steady beat is a challenge for toddlers. It seems like a simple movement: just pick up one foot and then the other. However, when you break down this task, a child must anticipate the beat of the song and pick up his foot in advance of the moment he is to put that foot down. This takes coordination and motor planning—and both are skills we want to give toddlers opportunities to practice and master. *Motor planning* is the child's ability to organize his motions in a purposeful way. To make walking to the beat easier, have him move forward. Play "follow the leader" with the song or make a path for him "through the forest" made of dish towels on your carpet.

♪ More Musical Fun with *Grizzly Bear*

● "Grizzly Bear" is a *ballad*—a song that tells a story, creating pictures in the child's mind. The ability to comprehend actions and events that cannot be seen is an important prelude to reading. The spoken words at the conclusion to this song were added to share with the listener that the SCARY bear is in fact a small child who is loved and adored by his parent. Ask your toddler if he is your little bear. Give him a bear hug, and pet or touch his "long, long HAIR" and point to his "big EYES" as you sing the "Grizzly Bear" song.

● Perhaps your child would like to climb under your CHAIR after the "long, long HAIR" verse. Then you can say the words to your little bear as he listens to the recording from under your chair. Peek under the chair and sign upside down to your child. This is certain to make the grizzliest of little bears laugh out loud!

● Invite a stuffed teddy bear to play the part of the grizzly bear. Touch the bear's hair and eyes when you sing the last verse. Put the bear under the chair. Let your child hide the bear so that Mommy or Daddy can go "a-LOOKIN'" for that grizzly bear.

Keaton gently touches the bear's
"big blue eyes."

GAMES AND ACTIVITIES

♪ A Bear with Hair Is Under My Chair!

VOCABULARY PRACTICE: BEAR, CHAIR*, HAIR*

DEVELOPMENTAL BENEFITS: positional concepts (under, off, on), experience with rhyming words, imaginative play

MATERIALS: sturdy chair with legs that will accommodate a toddler beneath the seat

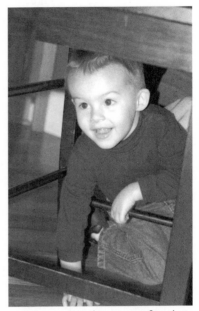

Stephen masters the concept of "under" from his perch beneath the chair.

DIRECTIONS: Place a sturdy chair in an open area for imaginative play. Play the "Grizzly Bear" song on your CD player. Sing and sign along with your child. Ask your child if he would like to climb under MOMMY'S CHAIR during the narration of the conclusion ("Hey, Little Bear . . ."). As you are telling the story with the narrator, be sure to reach under the chair and give your little bear a tickle.

Continue the game by asking your bear to: climb *on* the chair, climb *off* the chair, or walk *around* the chair. *Be certain to hold the chair steady so that it doesn't tip over.* If the chair is stable or you are willing to lay it on its side, the child can also climb *over* the chair. Awareness of *positional concepts* helps your toddler to understand words such as "off," "on," and "under" that describe where things are placed in relationship to a fixed object.

Your child may not be able to say a series of rhyming words such as "BEAR-HAIR-CHAIR," but will be an attentive listener. He will likely think your talking "game" is funny, and will begin to process which sounds remain the same and which sounds change in words to make them rhyme.

Incorporate imaginative play by asking your toddler: "What does the BEAR say?" If he makes a sound, pretend to be AFRAID of your little BEAR with your best terrified facial expression and dramatic AFRAID sign. Hug your "scary bear" and show him with your happy facial expression that you are no longer afraid of him!

---

* These bonus signs are found in the *Toddler Sing & Sign* Dictionary (page 207).

♪ Bear Skin Rug

VOCABULARY PRACTICE: **BEAR, BIG, LITTLE***

DEVELOPMENTAL BENEFITS: imaginative play, tactile stimulation, exploring same and different, labeling things that are big and little, positional concepts (under, over, on, off, around)

MATERIALS: two yards of brown fleece material, felt scraps, glue or needle and thread

Bear Skin Rug

DIRECTIONS: Make your toddler his own "bear skin" rug without inciting your local chapter of the Society for the Preservation of Long-Haired, Blue-Eyed Grizzly Bears. Use brown fleece material instead. You can make your rug as small or as large as you would like. And if you are feeling ambitious, you can make two rugs—one BIG and one LITTLE.

Make a pattern out of newspaper similar in shape to the pattern below. Using a marker, trace around the pattern onto the brown fleece material. Cut out your bear, and then cut fringe approximately three inches long at one-inch intervals all the way around the outer edge of the rug. To finish the edge, tie two adjacent pieces of fringe in a square knot. Repeat this process until the entire outer edge of the rug has been knotted. Complete by gluing or sewing felt to create the ears, eyes, nose, and mouth of your bear.

Ask your child if he would like to play with the bear. Let him play without direction, praising him for playing with the bear. Ask your child if he would like a bear hug. Wrap him in the rug, running your hands over your snug bear from head to toe. The pressure of your hands, in combination with the wonderful feel of the fleece against his skin, is very comforting and promotes *tactile,* or "touch," stimulation. This strategy also helps some children to get control of themselves if they are upset or overstimulated. A bear hug from his special rug may provide the comfort and coziness your child needs from time to time to help him sort out his emotions.

Ask your child to help the bear give you a hug. Allow your child to wrap you in the bear blanket. Lay the rug on the floor and take turns lying on the rug with your arms spread

* These bonus signs are found in the *Toddler Sing & Sign* Dictionary (page 207).

wide just like the bear. Ask your child to crawl *under* the bear. Then ask him to try walking *over* and around, or jumping *on* and *off* the bear rug.

You can make two rugs—BIG and LITTLE—so that you and your child can each have a bear hug. Have your child tell you with her signs which bear is BIG and which one is LITTLE. Your bear rug will be "beary" much fun!

♪ Growling Grizzly Treats

VOCABULARY PRACTICE: BEAR, BROWN

DEVELOPMENTAL BENEFITS: fine-motor skills, following step-by-step directions, sequencing

MATERIALS: one slice of bread, peanut butter, banana slices, raisins, plastic knife, paper plate

DIRECTIONS: Toast one slice of bread to use as a bear's face, and spread with peanut butter or butter. Cut banana slices to form the ears and snout and place on the toast. Give your child raisins to make the eyes and mouth. Allow your toddler to spread the sticky peanut butter on the bread. Show him where to place the banana pieces and raisins to form the bear's facial features. Repeat this activity a different day and see if your child remembers the *sequence* or order of steps for creating his bear treat.

Isaac prepares to gobble his Growling Grizzly Treat.

Ask him: "Where are BEAR's EYES?" Continue the game for ears, nose, and mouth. Tell him: "Your BEAR is BROWN!" Pretend to hide the "bear" with a paper plate and uncover it with great flourish. Ask him: "What color is your BEAR?" Repeat this hide-the-bear game and see if, with repetition, he will able to tell you the color of his yummy bear with his signs or spoken words.

A SIGN OF SUCCESS

♪ SIGN LANGUAGE CONTINUES TO BENEFIT CHILDREN ♪ AS THEY BEGIN TO WALK AND TALK

When I was born I was so surprised I didn't talk for a year and a half.

—GRACIE ALLEN (1906–1964)

Singing and signing can help babies transition into toddlerhood by allowing them to communicate their wants and needs to the caring adults in their world. Sign language enables toddlers to make choices, to make their opinions and desires known, to be heard. Sign language, music, and play support the healthy development of these age-appropriate ambitions.

Lettie began the *Baby Sing & Sign* program when she was seven months old. Her mother, Mandy, consistently incorporated the songs, signs, and playful activities into their daily life as a family. Lettie's first sign was MUSIC. Mandy observed, "I think she was fascinated by the fact that when I went to turn on the music on one side of the room, the music came out of a speaker on the other side of the room. She would just study the corner where the speaker was located with an amazed look on her face, because she couldn't actually see the speaker."

Mandy always said words as she signed to Lettie, offering plenty of praise and encouragement for Lettie's signing efforts, and progressed slowly in introducing new signed words. Lettie picked ones that were needs based (CEREAL, EAT, HELP) as well as words that were important to her (DOG, MUSIC). Mandy found that sign language supported Lettie's language development, because it is visual in nature. It made learning words for expressing concepts and experiences concrete, and easier for her daughter to understand.

> Sign language enables toddlers to make choices, to make their opinions and desires known, to be heard.

Lettie began to walk at ten months, but her sign language vocabulary continued to grow through her first birthday. By then she was using twenty to thirty signed words to express herself. Mandy believes that her daughter's *learning curve*—her rate of progress for mastering sign language skills—peaked at around the time she began to walk, and that their ability to communicate with each other eased Lettie's transition into the toddler stage.

Sign language supported Lettie's emerging speech even after she began combining words into sentences. If she said something her parents could not understand—or something that sounded like another word—she could then perform the sign to tell her parents exactly what she meant. "'Dadda' and 'cracker' used to sound alike when she first started saying 'cracker,' but she would sign when she said 'cracker' and I knew what she was saying."

Signing is a family affair with Lettie and her parents.

Mandy could also help Lettie with word choices when she was not certain what Lettie had said. She would sign two words for her daughter and ask her: "Did you say CAR or CAKE?" Lettie could then sign the word she had spoken—or look at Mom in puzzlement because she hadn't said either one of the words Mom guessed.

Toddlers are typically well on their way to acquiring speech. They have already accomplished many of the prerequisite skills, including:

- Listening to and understanding spoken words
- Figuring out that conversation requires two people to take turns in communicating
- Focusing their attention on the faces and fingers of those who sign and speak to them

As a caring adult, you can support new language learning with your toddler by:

- Accepting an *approximation,* or best try, when your child speaks or signs
- Encouraging your child to "tell me with your hands AND your voice" so that you are better able to decipher the meaning of the word he is trying to communicate
- Signing and speaking or singing many words to your toddler, creating the richest language environment possible for him
- Understanding that even though your toddler is very busy and on the move, he still picks up some of your sign language efforts through his peripheral vision. He may not appear to be paying attention, but he is a clever toddler and is benefiting more than you may realize.

Lettie is now eighteen months old and is talking in sentences. She still uses her familiar signs and learns new ones. The transition from sign to speech has been a gradual process as she has become more adept in articulating her spoken words. She uses signs for words that are difficult for her to say or for grasping new concepts, such as words for colors or feelings. She also loves her CRACKER sign and continues to use that gesture with her spoken word to make it perfectly clear that she needs a cracker, pronto!

Mandy noticed that Lettie picked up words and concepts more quickly when music was involved in the process. She is a firm believer in the benefit of *Baby Sing & Sign* for jump-starting her child's love of both language and music. Mandy recently gave birth to a little boy; and Lettie loves to entertain the baby with her songs and signs. Lettie is especially eager for the baby to learn the sign for MUSIC.

BOOKS TO READ

It's one thing to sing and sign about bears. But what if one visited you in your bed in the middle of the night while you were fast asleep? *Goodnight Lulu* by Paulette Bogan (Bloomsbury USA Children's Books) tells the story of a wide-eyed little chicken who wonders what would happen if dangerous—and not so dangerous—creatures were to invade her bedroom at night. Reminiscent of *The Runaway Bunny* by Margaret Wise Brown, this book reminds me of all the nights I would say good night to my boys, only to have them ask "one more thing"—or "fing"—depending on their speech proficiency. In true "Mommy Power" fashion, the momma hen describes the lengths to which she would go to keep her little chick safe.

And don't worry: even the bear gets a cozy night's sleep.

BROWN

Brown Bear, Brown Bear, What Do You See? By Bill Martin Jr. and Eric Carle (Henry Holt)

Brown Rabbit's Shape Book by Alan Baker (Kingfisher)

Moo Moo, Brown Cow by Jakki Wood (Red Wagon Books)

Pretty Brown Face by Andrea Davis Pinkney (Red Wagon Books)

Where Does the Brown Bear Go? by Nicki Weiss (Greenwillow Books)

LOOK/SEE

I See by Helen Oxenbury (Random House)

I See by Rachel Isadora (HarperCollins)

Look, Look! by Peter Linenthal (Dutton Juvenile)

Look! Look! Look! by Nancy Elizabeth Wallace and Linda K. Friedlaender (Marshall Cavendish Children's Books)

What Do You See? Come Look with Me: My First Lift-the-Flap Word Search Book by Sian Tucker (Little Simon)

SCARED/AFRAID

Go Away, Big Green Monster! by Ed Emberley (Little, Brown)

Off to School, Baby Duck by Amy Hest (Candlewick Press)

The Little Old Lady Who Was Not Afraid of Anything by Linda Williams and Megan Lloyd (HarperCollins)

The Owl Who Was Afraid of the Dark by Jill Tomlinson (Candlewick Press)

There's Something in My Attic by Mercer Mayer (Puffin Pied Piper Books)

3

THE CRAWDAD SONG

ANIMAL WORDS TO LEARN: **CRAWDAD, DOG**
COLOR WORD TO LEARN: **PINK**
OTHER WORDS TO LEARN: **GLAD/HAPPY, MAD/ANGRY, BABY, SUN,
MUD/DIRTY, HUG/LOVE**
WORDS TO REVIEW: **MOMMY*, DADDY*, SIT/CHAIR***
BONUS WORDS: **SAD*, MONSTER***

Crawdads look like little lobsters and can be found in most Southern streams. This song originates from children's play-party dances as well as from tunes sung by the workers building levees along the lower Mississippi River.

Chorus:

You get a line, I'll get a pole, honey;	*Clap hands*
You get a line, I'll get a pole, babe,	
You get a line, I'll get a pole,	
We'll all go fishin' in the CRAWDAD hole,	*Sign* CRAWDAD
Honey, BABY mine.	*Sign* BABY

Verse 1:

SITTIN' on the bank,	
With my DOG named Blue, honey,	*Sign* DOG
SITTIN' on the bank,	
With my DOG named Blue, babe,	*Sign* DOG
SITTIN' on the bank,	
With my DOG named Blue,	*Sign* DOG
Maybe he'll catch a CRAWDAD, too,	*Sign* CRAWDAD
Honey, BABY mine	

---

* These bonus signs are found in the *Toddler Sing & Sign* Dictionary (page 207).

Verse 2:
What-cha gonna do,
If the SUN don't shine, honey,   *Sign SUN*
What-cha gonna do,
If the SUN don't shine, babe?   *Sign SUN*
What-cha gonna do,
If the SUN don't shine?   *Sign SUN*
PLAY in the MUD and have a real good time . . . *Sign MUD/DIRTY*

Verse 3:
What-cha gonna do if your
MOMMA gets MAD, honey . . .   *Sign MAD/ANGRY*
Kiss her and HUG her until she's GLAD . . .   *Sign HUG/LOVE*

Verse 4:
The MOMMA and the DADDY,   *Sign BABY*
And the BABY makes three, honey . . .   *Sign BABY*
That's a CRAWDAD family . . .   *Sign CRAWDAD*

THE CRAWDAD SONG

Traditional / Adapted by Anne Meeker Miller

CRAWDAD

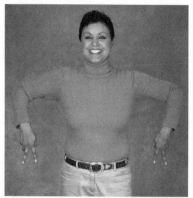

With elbows lifted, two open fingers of both hands form "claws" of crawdad by opening and closing.

Child may open and close hands without lifting elbows.

DOG

Pat leg as if calling a dog.

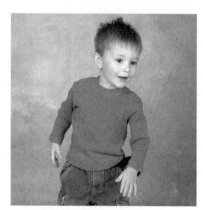

Child may pat one or both legs.

PINK

Place thumb between *two open fingers*, and move middle finger down across the lips to show their pink color.

Child may brush lips or chin with one or all fingers.

GLAD/HAPPY

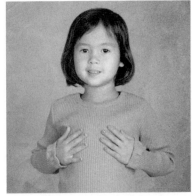

Open hands brush upward on chest
several times.

Child may pat chest with hands.

MAD/ANGRY

Curve *open hand* at face and
scrunch fingers.

Child may place *open hands* or *closed
fists* in front of face.

BABY

Rock arms as if holding a baby.

Child may place arms on tummy
and rock body.

SUN

Cup one hand and touch thumb to eyebrow.

Child may touch fingertips to head, or *cupped hand* to brow or cheek.

MUD/DIRTY

Place *open hand* under chin and wiggle fingers.

Child may tap chin with fingers.

HUG/LOVE

Place both *open hands* across chest, and squeeze arms as if hugging self (HUG).

Place both *closed fists* across chest (LOVE).

Child will likely hug self for both **HUG** and **LOVE** signs.

TIPS FOR INTRODUCING *THE CRAWDAD SONG*

○ It is a scientific fact that toddlers prefer songs with quick and lively tempos. "The Crawdad Song" certainly moves lickety-split with its bluegrass instruments and driving beat. Please do not try to sign every word in the lyrics. Select a few signs to support the key words in this musical story such as CRAWDAD and DOG. If you would like, you can add more signs gradually as you become familiar with the song.

○ Start by "putting the beat" in your hands or feet with a clap or stomp. Listen together to the story told with each verse of the song. After you have listened to the song several times, clap or stomp during the chorus ("You get a line, I'll get a pole, honey . . .") and listen to the words of the story during the verses ("Sittin' on the bank with my DOG named Blue . . .").

○ When your child is familiar with the song, try signing only the word CRAWDAD each time you hear it in the music. Sing or say the single word "crawdad" as you sign CRAWDAD.

○ Continue to add single words such as SUN or MAD/ANGRY as your child enjoys this musical story. He will begin to anticipate the events of the story and show you he comprehends their sequence by signing the key words before singing them. Praise this wonderful feat by saying, "Yes, dog named Blue! Good remembering what comes next, buddy."

○ Many caring adults—parents, caregivers, teachers—make the mistake of trying to sign too many words for the child to master or comprehend their connection to spoken words. Most eighth graders I know could not sign all of the key words in "The Crawdad Song" at its fast pace. When you are signing with children of any age, remember not to overwhelm them with the gestures at the expense of musical enjoyment and fun!

♪ More Musical Fun with *The Crawdad Song*

● Try clapping the chorus ("You get a line . . .") of the song, and stop to sign CRAWDAD at the end of the chorus when you sing, "We'll go down to the CRAWDAD hole." Your child may also like to sign BABY when they sing, "BABY mine."

- Take your toddler for a crawdad stroll by walking to the beat around a chair or table. Stop walking and sign CRAWDAD when you sing the last line of the chorus ("We'll go down to the CRAWDAD hole.")
- Use appropriate facial expressions for asking questions when you sing and sign, "What-cha gonna do if the SUN don't shine?" or "What-cha gonna do if your MOMMA gets mad?" Lift your eyebrows and tilt your head. Help your child practice his facial expressions by asking him to "show me your HAPPY face." He can also look at his own facial expression in a mirror to learn how to express his feelings on his face. Make sure you are modeling the facial expressions yourself. Repeat for MAD and SAD expressions. These feelings are more challenging for your child to convey.

Maizie signs CRAWDAD with both
thumbs and pointer fingers.

GAMES AND ACTIVITIES

♪ Crawdad Cuisine

VOCABULARY PRACTICE: CRAWDAD, MUD/DIRTY, GLAD/HAPPY, SAD*, SIT/CHAIR*

DEVELOPMENTAL BENEFITS: sensory exploration, fine-motor control, attention to task, perseverance

MATERIALS: 9 x 13–inch metal cake pan; two cups of chocolate pudding (ready-made or homemade); marshmallows, teddy bear cookies and/or any other small favorite snack food, such as bite-sized pieces of fruit, yogurt-covered raisins; small plastic ice tongs, appetizer tongs, strawberry hullers, or any other small tong that is easy to manipulate; small bowl; placemat; bib or old shirt; high chair or booster seat at a regular-sized table or child-sized chair and child-sized table; washcloth or paper towels for cleanup

DIRECTIONS: Invite your child to the table to have a seat in his CHAIR. Place the cake pan on your child's placemat in front of him and add the pudding. Place a small empty bowl by the cake pan. Dress your child in a bib or old shirt, and allow him to toss marshmallows or other small snack items into the pudding.

To begin, explain to your child that he gets to be a CRAWDAD. Show him the sign and possibly a picture if you have one. (You can find pictures of almost anything using Google and searching its image files.) It is mealtime and the crawdad is very hungry! But there is a problem: crawdads don't have hands. They only have pinchers (claws). Explain to your child that he can use only his pinchers to get the snack that is hiding down in the MUD pudding where CRAWDADS like to live.

Demonstrate how to open and close the tongs and how to use them to retrieve a snack from the MUD pudding and place it in the small bowl. Act a little bit SAD when a snack is dropped, and act extremely HAPPY when it is "caught" and placed in the bowl. After your child has retrieved several snacks, he can take a break and eat his "catch of the day." Add more snacks to the MUD pudding and try again. (If your child is having trouble getting the snack to the bowl, bring the bowl closer or hold it right under his tongs for him after he snags his catch.)

* These bonus signs are found in the *Toddler Sing & Sign* Dictionary (page 207).

Sing and sign "The Crawdad Song" as you retrieve the snacks. Be silly and have fun. Join your child in retrieving the snacks. Crawdad mommies and daddies get hungry, too. The fine-motor control that is needed to master the tongs is tricky. Being silly helps take the "work" out of the fine-motor task for your child.

After mastering the tongs, it may be fun for your child to try to use his own "pinchers" to retrieve his snack. Show your child the sign for CRAWDAD and how to open and shut your pointer and middle fingers. Now try to use fingers "pinchers" to retrieve the snacks. Once a snack is "caught," eat it immediately.

Now it's time to get really messy! Talk and laugh about how DIRTY your hands are getting. Take time to lick them clean. YUM! You can add toys that have been thoroughly washed to the mud for play extensions, too. Spoons and scoops will be very handy when your crawdad gets tired and needs some fast and easy crawdad fuel. Let him scoop up his snack right from the pan. Ice cream cones make wonderful scoops and can be a very fun way to end this activity. Your child can scoop and eat individual bites, or he can use the spoon to fill the cone and then eat his "Mud Pudding Crawdad Cone" as the grand finale.

Who knew crawdads had so much fun?

The tongs work like a crawdad's pinchers
and provide great fine-motor practice
as Michael finds the marshmallows
in the pudding.

♪ Pretty in Pink (And Other Colors, Too!)

VOCABULARY PRACTICE: color words, including **PINK** and **BROWN; BABY; MUD/DIRTY; HAPPY; MAD/ANGRY**

DEVELOPMENTAL BENEFITS: tactile sensory experience, problem solving, imaginary play

MATERIALS: three yards of a variety of colors of tulle netting, including pink and brown (sold at Wal-Mart or other fabric store)

Maizie and Maia play "hide and seek" with tulle netting.

DIRECTIONS: Tulle netting is very inexpensive and is ideal for peek-a-boo or other sensory games, because it is sheer and your toddler can see through the fabric. Take the length of fabric and wrap it around your child or drape it loosely over his head. Say, "Has anyone seen my BABY, [child's name]? I have no idea where he is. I have LOOKED everywhere and he's gone! I am so SAD." Make a show of using your most pitiful, sad face for your child to see. If your toddler hasn't already taken the netting off of himself, unwrap or uncover him with great flourish and say, "There you are, [child's name]! I am so HAPPY to see you. Look at my HAPPY face!"

You can play a variation of this game using various colors of the tulle netting. Wrap him in the pink netting and announce to him that you are looking for a PINK BABY. Ask him if he has seen a PINK BABY anywhere. He will inevitably start unwrapping himself, and you can feign surprise that you have fortunately discovered a pink baby in your own living room. Repeat the game with other colors of tulle.

You can also encourage imaginative play with the tulle netting to incorporate the MUD/DIRTY sign. Wrap your toddler in brown netting, and pretend that he has gotten very dirty and is covered in mud! Sing "The Crawdad Song" verse: "What-cha gonna do if your MOMMA gets MAD?" and tickle, bounce, or hug him as you sing with your arms wrapped around your "muddy" toddler. Then give him a good "scrub" to "clean him up" by taking off his brown tulle—and tickling and hugging him some more. *Supervise your child's tulle game, and put the tulle away for another day of play when you have finished the activity.*

♪ Happy/Sad Paper Plate Mask

VOCABULARY PRACTICE: **HAPPY, SAD*, DADDY*, MOMMY***
DEVELOPMENTAL BENEFITS: problem solving, exploration of feelings
MATERIALS: two paper plates, tongue depressor, newspaper, stapler, masking or plastic tape or a "foamie mask" (available at craft stores), magazines or digital camera and printer

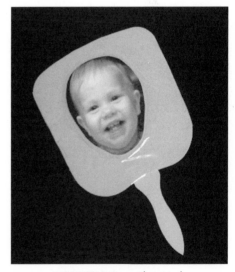

HAPPY/SAD Paper Plate Mask

DIRECTIONS: Tape a tongue depressor "lollipop style" between two paper plates. Stuff the space between the paper plates with newspaper to prevent collapse. Staple the plates together, and cover the staples with masking or plastic tape. You could also purchase a "foamie mask" made of foam core with the handle already attached. The photograph shows a mask made using a "foamie mask."

Print copies of two digital photographs of an important person in your toddler's life: parent, sibling, friend or caregiver. In one photograph, the person should demonstrate a "sad" facial expression, and in the other, a "happy" one. You can also cut "happy" and "sad" pictures out of a magazine. Affix a picture of the SAD image on one side of the plate mask and a HAPPY image on the other side. You can also cover the pictures with clear Con-Tact paper to make the toy more "toddler-proof."

Ask your child if he would like to play the HAPPY-SAD game. Hold up the mask and ask him to touch the HAPPY side. Tell him: "Daddy is HAPPY. Look at his

---

* These bonus signs are found in the *Toddler Sing & Sign* Dictionary (page 207).

HAPPY eyes and his HAPPY mouth. Touch his HAPPY face." Repeat for the sad photograph. After he has enjoyed this game, allow him to hold the toy and ask him, "Where is HAPPY Daddy?" See if he will find the happy photograph and show it to you. Repeat for sad Daddy.

Toddlers love to look at the faces of other toddlers and especially their own face! Give your child practice in imitating your facial expression for HAPPY and SAD. When he is able to produce facial expressions that approximate HAPPY and SAD, take his photograph. Print these precious pictures and make another mask. Make a new mask with your toddler's photographs again next month—you'll be amazed at how much more precise and communicative that sweet little face becomes with age and experience.

A SIGN OF SUCCESS

♪ CHILDHOOD FEARS: HOW TO HELP TODDLERS HANDLE ♪ THINGS THAT GO BUMP IN THE NIGHT

No matter how old you are, you always think that there may be something hiding under your bed.

—SARAH, AGE 5

Order now while supplies last: Anne's amazing Monster-Be-Gone Spray! It is guaranteed to ward off all scary things with one liberal application, including any ghoul, giant, Tyrannosaurus rex, jungle animal, ominous vacuum cleaner, or weird space traveler that may wander in through your front door or backyard. Be the first on your block to have a carefree, fear-free family life. Your toddler will thank you.

Please don't tell my son Andy, but my monster spray was actually air freshener. My eighteen-month-old was convinced that a band of monsters had taken up residence in our side yard. As the sun set, his angst began to elevate. In his fearful toddler mind, the monsters multiplied exponentially after dark.

I sent his father to the side yard one evening around Andy's bedtime to commence with the Monster Extermination Procedure. My husband sprayed enthusiastically (and with great personal style) while Andy and I watched through the window. (I should mention that my spouse was as fragrant as a rosebush for weeks following this exercise.) After the spraying exorcism in our side yard, I was truly amazed at how quickly our specific variety of side yard monsters became a nonissue for Andy. It was in acknowledging Andy's fear and confronting it together as a family that we managed to send all of our boy's monsters packing.

A healthy dose of fear is a good thing—our fight-or-flight response allows us to immediately react to threatening situations. But what about our response to danger that is not actually present?

Researchers at New York University believe that the human brain responds to fear that is perceived but not actually present in the same way it does if something bad actually happens to a person, like, for instance, being bitten by a snake or struck by lightning. In studying the structures of the brain, Richard Thompson, a neuroscientist, found evidence that our brain judges and responds similarly to events we imagine to be a real threat and those we learn to fear through experience.

> By acknowledging our child's fear and confronting it together as a family, we managed to send all of our boy's monsters packing.

Can we say without hesitation that monsters are not real? I hope so. Can we tell a toddler that his fears are not real? Not a good idea, according to family counselors Eileen Paris, PhD, and Thomas Paris, PhD, who encourage us to validate a toddler's fright by mirroring the child's intensity with our own words and vocal quality. "You are really scared of monsters, Andy! You worry that there may be monsters in our yard!" You can then follow this empathetic response with assurances that you will keep him safe and that everything will be fine.

Your toddler is beginning to develop an active imagination and memory for experiences—particularly the fearful ones—in his short life thus far. His newfound mobility makes it possible for him to travel farther away from the security of caring and trusted adults. He is self-centered enough to believe that anything bad that could happen to another person will likely happen to him as well.

The good news is that sign language can be a useful tool for allaying your toddler's fears. Here are some ideas to help:

○ **Name your child's fear.** Pair the word with the sign and give your child the ability to tell you what he fears. You can then deal specifically with the object or experience that worries him. Use an ASL book or Web site video dictionary to find the sign you are looking for. By Googling "video dictionary," you will find an array of Web sites to help you find the ASL sign you are looking for.

○ **The particular thing that goes bump in the night at your house might not be cooperative enough to be found in a dictionary.** Eighteen-month-old Sam was terrified that "Hoopy" would snatch him from his cozy bed some night. In this case, you might choose a sign with a similar meaning, like MONSTER, or you might help your child come up with a unique sign for his "ghoulie." The sign for MONSTER is found in the *Toddler Sing & Sign* Dictionary (page 207).

○ **Give your toddler a tool to protect him from his fear.** Give him a small child-proof flashlight or night-light to illuminate the corners of his room. Perhaps you could instruct a stuffed animal to stand guard and protect your child from his fearful object or experience. If the lawn mower is what scares him most, then purchase a small toy one and let him help you mow the yard.

○ **Read books together that present a warm and fuzzy version of your toddler's feared object or experience, and sign that object or experience together.**

Andy loved the book *There's Something in My Attic* by Mercer Mayer (Puffin Books). Mayer introduces us to a brave little girl armed with a flashlight and lasso who captures a monster in the attic. She discovers that the scary guy simply wants to cuddle her teddy bear, because he is lonely sleeping all by himself. Your child will identify with the monster, realizing that perhaps he and the monster have some feelings—and fears—in common. With the infinite variety of picture books available, you are certain to find one that can help you discuss your toddler's fear with humor and empathy.

○ **Give your child the "heads-up" when you are likely to encounter the feared object or experience.** Toddlers don't have the same ability to control their environment to avoid things that frighten them as adults do. If elephants terrify him, steer clear of them when you visit the zoo, or prepare him as you visit the other animals first. If bugs are his "bugaboo," then remind him that you may see some bugs at the park today, but that you will shoo them away from your toddler. Warning your toddler by using familiar words and signs gives him the chance to organize his feelings and calm himself.

Most children outgrow these typical toddler fears by the time they reach three to four years of age. If your child is inconsolable or is consistently and continually afraid, he may have developed a phobia. In this situation, it would be wise to contact your pediatrician for advice.

Small children inhabit a big and often frightening world. Hold your toddler, console him, and share with him that you were once a little person with big fears, too.

Dad comforts fearful Eleanor with reassuring words and kisses.

BOOKS TO READ

What can we do to cheer a sad child? That is a question we as parents are constantly trying to answer. A menagerie of animal friends set about the task of comforting an unhappy child in *What Shall We Do with the Boo-Hoo Baby?* by Cressida Cowell and Ingrid Godon (Scholastic). Using teamwork, the cast of critters finally solves the mystery of why the baby is in distress.

CRAWDAD

Baby Einstein: Who Lives in the Pond? by Julie Aigner-Clark (Baby Einstein)

Down at the Pond by Lorraine Long (Periwinkle Park Educational Productions)

Hello Hello by Dan Zanes (Little, Brown Young Readers)

In the Small, Small Pond by Denise Fleming (Henry Holt)

Pond by Lizi Boyd (Chronicle Books)

DOG

Bingo by Rosemary Wells (Scholastic)

Doggies: A Counting and Barking Book by Sandra Boynton (Little Simon)

Dog's Noisy Day by Emma Dodd (Dutton Books)

Go, Dog, Go! by P. D. Eastman (Random House Books for Young Readers)

Please, Puppy, Please! by Spike Lee and Tonya Lewis Lee (Simon & Schuster)

PINK

Double Pink by Kate Feiffer (Simon & Schuster/Paula Wiseman Books)

Little Pink Pig by Pat Hutchins (Greenwillow Books)

My Many Colored Days by Dr. Seuss (Alfred A. Knopf)

Pink Piglets by Roger Generazzo (Golden Books)

Pink, Red, Blue, What Are You? by Laura McGee Kvasnosky (Dutton Children's Books)

GLAD/HAPPY

Glad Monster, Sad Monster by Ed Emberly and Anne Miranda (Little, Brown)

I Feel Happy and Sad and Angry and Glad by Mary Elizabeth Murphy (DK Children)

If You're Happy and You Know It by Annie Kubler (Child's Play International)

Little Teddy Bear's Happy Face/Sad Face by Lynn Offerman (Millbrook Press)

The Happy Book: Touch and Feel Fun for Every Little One by Diane Muldrow (Cartwheel Books)

MAD/ANGRY

Alexander and the Terrible, Horrible, No Good, Really Bad Day by Judith Viorst and Ray Cruz (Aladdin)

Happy, Mad, Silly, Sad by Dennis Full (Scholastic)

I Feel Angry by Marcia Leonard (Candy Cane Press)

I Was So Mad by Mercer Mayer (Golden Books)

When You're Mad and You Know It by Elizabeth Crary (Parenting Press)

BABY

Baby Cakes by Karma Wilson (Little Simon)

Baby Faces by DK Publishing (DK Publishing)

Everywhere Babies by Susan Meyers and Marla Frazee (Red Wagon Books)

Hush, Little Baby by Marla Frazee (Voyager Books)

I Kissed the Baby by Mary Murphy (Candlewick Press)

SUN

Goodnight Sun, Hello Moon by Reader's Digest (Reader's Digest)

I Love You, Sun, I Love You, Moon by Tomie dePaola (Putnam Juvenile)

Warm Sun, Soft Sand by Linzi West (Frances Lincoln)

What Can You Do in the Sun? by Anna Grossnickle Hines (Greenwillow Books)

What the Sun Sees, What the Moon Sees by Nancy Tafuri (Greenwillow Books)

MUD/DIRTY

Duck Is Dirty by Satoshi Kitamura (Farrar, Straus and Giroux)

Harry the Dirty Dog by Gene Zion (HarperCollins)

I'm Dirty by Kate and Jim McMullan (Joanna Cotler)

Mrs. Wishy-Washy by Joy Cowley and Elizabeth Fuller (Philomel)

The Piggy in the Puddle by Charlotte Pomerantz (Aladdin)

HUG/LOVE

Counting Kisses: A Kiss and Read Book by Karen Katz (Little Simon)

I Love My Mommy by Sebastien Braun (HarperCollins)

I Love You, Little One by Nancy Tafuri (Scholastic)

I Love You Through and Through by Bernadette Rossetti-Shustak (Cartwheel Books)

Skidamarink! I Love You by Michael Scott (Hyperion Books for Children)

TINGALAYO

ANIMAL WORD TO LEARN: **DONKEY**
COLOR WORD TO LEARN: **GRAY**
OTHER WORDS TO LEARN: **EAT, PLAY, SLEEP**
WORDS TO REVIEW: **GLAD/HAPPY, RUN*, WALK***
BONUS WORDS TO LEARN: **TALK*, LAUGH*, WAKE*, KICK*,
CAKE*, BALL*, CEREAL*, CARROT*, HELP*, PLEASE***

"Tingalayo" is probably the best-known Caribbean children's song in the United States. Most versions include "me donkey walk, me donkey talk, me donkey eat with a knife and fork." The practice of improvising new lyrics that reflects daily work and play is common in Caribbean folk music.

Chorus:

Tingalayo, RUN me little DONKEY RUN,	*Sign DONKEY*
Tingalayo, RUN me little DONKEY RUN.	*Sign DONKEY*

Verse 1:

Me DONKEY WALK,	*Walk in place or pat thighs*
Me DONKEY TALK,	*Walk in place or pat thighs*
Me DONKEY EAT with a knife and fork . . .	*Sign EAT*

Verse 2:

Me DONKEY LAUGH,	*Smile!*
Me DONKEY PLAY,	*Sign PLAY*
Me DONKEY HAPPY each and every day . . .	*Sign HAPPY and smile!*

Verse 3:

Me DONKEY SLEEP,	*Sign SLEEP*
Me DONKEY WAKE,	*Clap hands*
Me DONKEY EAT the cho-co-la-te CAKE . . .	*Sign EAT*

---

* These bonus signs are found in the *Toddler Sing & Sign* Dictionary (page 207).

TINGALAYO

Traditional / Adapted by Anne Meeker Miller

DONKEY

Show movement of the "donkey's ears" by placing thumbs at temple and bending *closed hands*.

Child may touch head or face with fingertips or open hands.

GRAY

Flutter *two closed fingers* up and down.

Child may flutter closed hand or two open fingers up and down.

EAT/FOOD

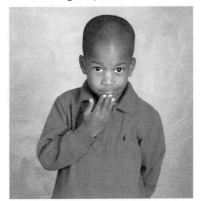

Tap *gathered fingers* to lips.

Child may place *open hand* on or in mouth.

PLAY

Extend thumb and little fingers of both *closed fists* and twist both at wrists.

Child may shake both *open hand*s repetitively.

SLEEP

Rest head on *closed hand* palm side up as if head rests on a pillow.

Child may place one or both hands on head and tap several times.

TIPS FOR INTRODUCING *TINGALAYO*

○ "Tingalayo" is a wonderful song for dancing. Introduce the song to your toddler by picking her up and spinning her around your kitchen or living room "dance floor." Twirl and dip your little dancer.

○ Tell your toddler that "Tingalayo" is the name of the donkey in the story. Sign DONKEY throughout the chorus. Your "donkey ears" can flap to the beat of the tune. Once she has mastered the sign, you can pat thighs or clap hands to the lyric "Tingalayo" and sign DONKEY as you sing, "RUN, me little DONKEY, RUN!"

○ Pantomime the lyrics of the verses, or add a steady beat with pats and claps. Sign the key words, such as EAT, PLAY, SLEEP, and HAPPY.

♪ More Musical Fun with *Tingalayo*

Rosie and Emery enjoy their kitchen "steel drums."

● Practice signing the key words during the parts in the song where only instruments are playing. Playfully repeat the same word over again, such as: "EAT, EAT, EAT, EAT," or combine words into short phrases, such as "DONKEY SLEEP, DONKEY SLEEP." Make a game of trying to entice your toddler into imitating your "silly signing" play!

● Try signing DONKEY when you hear "Tingalayo," as this is the donkey's name. Run in place on the lyrics "RUN, me little DONKEY, RUN!" Or you can travel around a stationary object, such as a chair, as you sing. Walk as you sign DONKEY for "Tingalayo," and then run as you sing, "RUN, me little donkey, RUN!" Play a game of "follow the leader" and take turns leading.

● Add "steel drums" to your singing by adding a kitchen band of pots and pans. Show your toddler how to play along with the instrumental interludes and sign when you hear the singers, or enjoy a complete performance of the "Tingalayo" song with steel drum accompaniment by your toddler.

GAMES AND ACTIVITIES

♪ Donkey Cake Bake

VOCABULARY PRACTICE: DONKEY, BIG, LITTLE*, CEREAL*, CARROT*

DEVELOPMENTAL BENEFITS: stimulation of touch and smell; estimation of large and small; fine-motor skills

MATERIALS: small and large bowl, small whisk or spoon, measuring cups, funnel, 9 x 13–inch baking pan

INGREDIENTS:

1¾ cups all-purpose flour

½ cup Quaker Unprocessed Bran cereal

2 teaspoons baking soda

2 teaspoons pumpkin pie spice or ground cinnamon

1 teaspoon salt

1½ cups sugar

¾ cup vegetable oil

3 eggs

2 cups shredded carrots

Cooking spray

½ cup golden raisins (optional)

Powdered sugar (optional)

DIRECTIONS: Donkeys love to eat cereal and carrots. This snack cake combines donkeys' favorite food groups for a treat that is healthy and delicious. Your toddler can help with the cake preparation and have a sensory-rich experience as well. Give her a big bowl filled with a small amount of oat bran cereal to run through her fingertips as you talk about what DONKEYS love to eat. Give her a small plastic funnel or cups to scoop and play in her bowl of oat cereal. Mix in a little of the cinnamon and/or pumpkin spice ingredients listed to give her sense of smell some stimulation as well. Let her mix the oats with a small whisk or spoon.

Give her a small bowl of shredded carrots. As she feels the CARROT pieces, she will probably notice the difference in texture—the wet, cool carrots will give her a tactile experience that contrasts with the warm, dry oat bran cereal. Talk to her

---

* These bonus signs are found in the *Toddler Sing & Sign* Dictionary (page 207).

about the different sizes of her two bowls of donkey food. Which one is BIG? Which one is LITTLE?

Converse with spoken and signed words about the donkey food as you prepare the snack cake together. Involve your toddler in the cake preparation by letting her dump the ingredients you have measured into the mixing bowl. She can also help stir the eggs and carrots into the batter. When the batter is in the pan, allow her to touch the mixture with her fingers. Give her a second touching opportunity when the cake has baked and cooled.

Feed your little toddler "donkey" a piece of the cake she helped to bake!

To complete your yummy Donkey Cake Bake, follow these instructions:

Matthew learns about texture with his fingertips by touching the wet carrots and the dry oatmeal.

1. Heat oven to 350° F. Spray a 9 x 13–inch baking pan with cooking spray.
2. In a medium bowl, combine flour, bran, baking soda, pumpkin pie spice, and salt; mix well. Set aside.
3. In a large bowl, beat sugar and oil on medium speed with an electric mixer. Add eggs, one a time, beating well after each addition.
4. Add dry ingredients; mix on low speed until blended. Stir in carrots. Add raisins if your child likes them.
5. Pour the batter into the pan. Bake 30 to 35 minutes or until a wooden toothpick inserted in the center comes out clean. Place the pan on a wire rack and cool completely. If desired, sprinkle the cake with powdered sugar.
6. Store tightly covered. Serves 12.

(This recipe for Carrot Snack Cake is reprinted by permission of the Quaker Oats Company.)

♪ Toddler Tails

VOCABULARY PRACTICE: DONKEY, GRAY, EAT, PLAY, SLEEP, GLAD/HAPPY, SAD*
DEVELOPMENTAL BENEFITS: imaginative play, exploration of feelings
MATERIALS: black knit cap. one gray and one pink or white felt square, needle and thread. black or gray athletic sock, polyfill stuffing, two feet of black or gray grosgrain ribbon, black or gray socks (optional)

This little "donkey" is ready for play!

DIRECTIONS: "Tingalayo" is a busy donkey. He likes many of the things your busy toddler enjoys: sleeping, eating, and playing. Toddlers love to pretend, and here is a simple way to transform your toddler into our HAPPY DONKEY, Tingalayo.

To make the donkey's tail, fill the athletic sock with polyfill stuffing. Sew the open end closed and stitch to the center of the grosgrain ribbon. Tie the ribbon loosely around your toddler's waist and let her get used to running, hopping, and dancing with a tail attached. Show your toddler how to "swish" his DONKEY tail by moving his hips.

To make donkey ears, cut two gray and two pink or white "ears" out of felt in the shape of the drawing on the next page. Place one gray piece on top of one pink or white piece, and, using needle and thread, sew around the edges of the ear. Turn the felt ear pieces inside out. Repeat to create a second ear. Sew the ears onto the knit cap.

---

* This bonus sign is found in the *Toddler Sing & Sign* Dictionary (page 207).

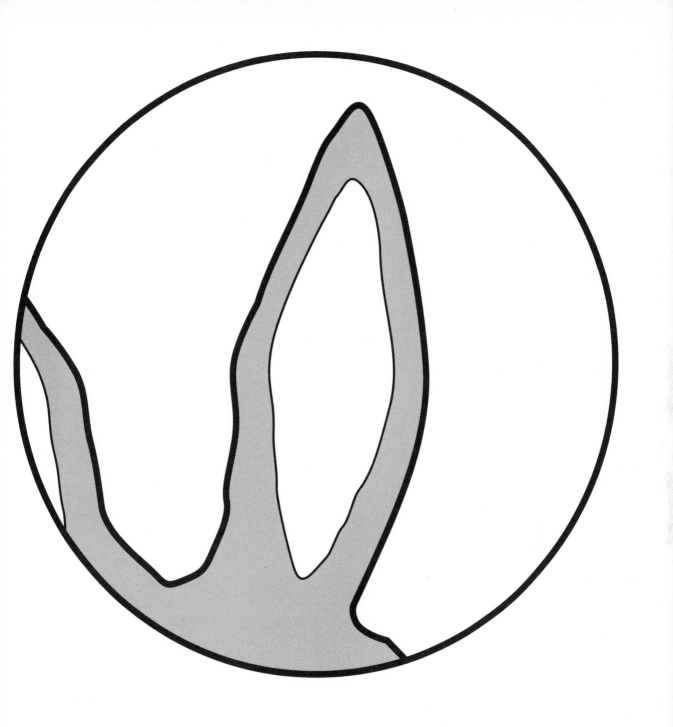

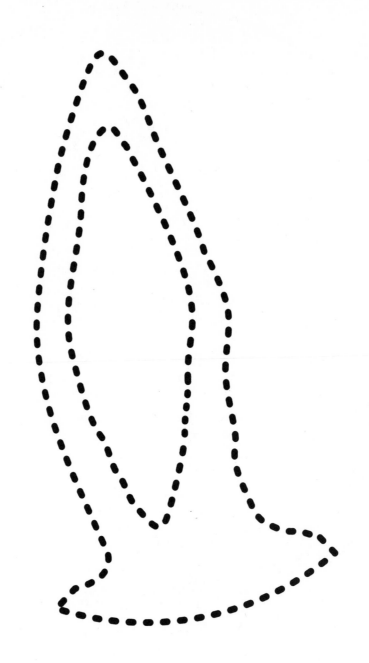

Help your toddler put on her donkey-ear cap and her tail. If you want to get fancy with your dress-up game, have your child put a pair of socks on her hands and let her try out her "hooves" for a while to see what it feels like to eat and play without opposable thumbs.

Sing the "Tingalayo" song with your toddler donkey. Pretend to feed her and put her to bed on the floor or couch. Tickle her when you sing: "Me donkey laughs." Tell her that she is your little donkey, and give her choices using signs: "Does my DONKEY want to EAT or SLEEP? LAUGH or PLAY? Is my DONKEY HAPPY or SAD?" Then join in the pretend play with your donkey!

♪ The Kicking DONKEY

VOCABULARY PRACTICE: DONKEY, PLAY, KICK*, BALL*

DEVELOPMENTAL BENEFITS: large-motor and motor-planning skills, balance, coordination

MATERIALS: balls of various sizes, weights, and textures for kicking (beach, playground, cloth, plastic, leather); balloon and string or yarn; laundry basket; paper; beanbags or pillows

DIRECTIONS: Both toddlers and donkeys love to kick up their heels! Have your little "donkey" sit on the floor with her hands on the floor behind her. Show her how to use both feet to KICK a beach BALL to you. It is also fun to tie a piece of string or yarn to a balloon and then have your toddler hold the string and kick the balloon. She may enjoy a game of "kick the ball into the laundry basket" with the basket positioned on its side like a soccer goal. Other fun things for "donkeys" to kick include balloons, wadded-up paper, beanbags placed on top of her foot, and pillows.

Use caution when allowing small children to play with balloons. A child who chews on a balloon when it pops can choke by inhaling it. *Make certain that your child is kicking the balloon and not putting it in her mouth.*

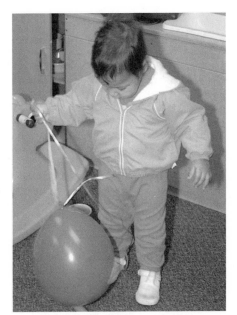

Kicking a balloon tied to a string is a great way for toddlers to practice their motor-planning skills.

* These bonus signs are found in the *Toddler Sing & Sign* Dictionary (page 207).

A SIGN OF SUCCESS
♪ TAMING TODDLER TANTRUMS ♪

"Who are you and what have you done with my sweet boy, Greggie Miller?"

These are my unspoken words to the screaming, writhing, hyperventilating "toddler terrorist" I carried out of the bookstore. I held him at arm's length to escape injury while he thrashed about. As I moved in slow motion past all of the Saturday morning customers who wanted nothing more than quiet and relaxation, I felt as if I were trying to jog through the deep end of a swimming pool carrying a bouncing bowling ball.

Tantrums happen. I have been known to throw a good one myself on occasion, but adults call it "venting." Tantrums are what earned toddlers their notorious reputation for being members of the crowd known as the Terrible Twos. However, in all fairness, toddlers don't have the savvy menu of appropriate behavioral alternatives to screaming and kicking that adults possess. They tend to forget rules, they are experiencing some new and not-so-cute emotions such as jealousy and shame, and they can exhibit their limited repertoire of emotional responses with an intensity that parallels a volcanic eruption. It is no wonder that "meltdown" is another word we attach to their seismic attacks of killer grumpiness.

What can you do to lessen the number and intensity of toddler tantrums? Fortunately, sign language has proven a useful means of calming these storms.

It is important to remember the triggers that most often precede a toddler's tantrum. The short list includes frustration, hunger, and fatigue. An often-cited source of frustration for toddlers is their inability to communicate their wants and needs. In this scenario, frustration can be short-circuited easily with sign language. Genevieve, the mother of eighteen-month-old Tabitha, relates: "When our daughter was unable to talk, learning how to sign was like the magic pill for preventing tantrums. She was able to communicate what she needed without getting frustrated. Since Tabitha learned how to sign, she has not once thrown a tantrum because we did not understand her."

Bob agrees, as he has observed his sixteen-month-old daughter, Alexis, grow more confident and resourceful in her decision-making skills as her sign language facility increased.

I feel as though Alexis's capability to communicate with us has helped curb meltdowns and tantrums. Don't get me wrong: she still has some! After all, they are important to a child's development in moderation. But Alexis whines and cries far less than many toddlers we know. We are always complimented on how well behaved she is. I think this stems from our ability to communicate with one another. When she needs some independent time, she is able to find things to do by herself in our home. When she is ready for our company, she will sign PLAY while verbalizing "Daddy play."

My son Greg once launched into a temper tantrum primarily because I did not give him the thing he wanted: a new picture book. I applaud his valiant effort to sway my decision-making skills, compromised as they were at that moment by the decibel level of his screams. However, had I succumbed and bought him the book he desired in order to stop him from screeching, I would have taught him that having a tantrum is the perfect solution to get what you want.

Dr. Harvey Karp, a pediatrician and author of *The Happiest Toddler on the Block,* cautions that your toddler makes subconscious notes as to the outcomes of his tantrums. According to Karp, "It's not conscious manipulation. It's more like a habit he keeps finding himself falling back into." The key to avoiding this particularly worrisome type of toddler tantrum is to consistently and calmly stick to your guns. Pride yourself in the fact that there isn't a scream piercing enough or a kicking foot swift enough to deter you from your role as parent, teacher, and protector of your child. It's a big job with big rewards. However, the return on your investment in time and patience may feel like it is taking awhile to materialize.

> It is important to remember the triggers that most often precede a toddler's tantrum. The short list includes frustration, hunger, and fatigue. Sign language can help alleviate these triggers.

In the meantime, here are some tips for helping your frustrated child:

○ Dr. Karp suggests that you respond to your child's aggravation with empathy, and mirror the source of her frustration as well as the intensity of her feelings in your conversation. ("You want to climb into your high chair without my help! You like doing things all by yourself!")

○ Remind your toddler to "use your words" to sign HELP or PLEASE when she needs you to lend her a hand. These sign are found in *the Toddler Sing & Sign Dictionary* (page 207).

○ Get on her level in order to make eye contact so that she feels you are fully present in her moment of need.

○ Break down the task she is attempting to do on her own into smaller chunks, and support her to get each minitask accomplished.

Sign language can also assist a hungry or tired child in communicating her displeasure before the event of a full-scale temper tantrum. Myra noticed that using sign language helped her and her husband know when their toddler daughter, Adelina, was hungry, tired, or hurt. "We taught her the signs for EAT, SLEEP, and HELP, and Adelina then used the words appropriately to communicate what she was feeling. I believe this has alleviated much of her crying and need to throw tantrums to get what she wants. Since she could tell us what she needed at such a young age, there wasn't a need for her to get upset and for us to play guessing games all the time."

The inability to communicate is certainly frustrating, and that frustration can be compounded by a toddler's passionate desire to do things all by herself ("Me do!"). Give her opportunities to practice her decision-making skills and enjoy a little bit of the independence she desires—but within limits. Give her choices, involve her in your conversations, and praise her for making decisions that keep her safe. Amy gives her two-year-old son, Gianni, as many choices as she can each day: *Do you want applesauce or peaches, the dog book or the car book, my left or my right hand as we cross the parking lot together, the blue pajamas or the green ones?* Her generosity in giving Gianni input on the decisions in his life makes it easier when she needs to take over some of the necessary, more important decisions for her son.

Don't fall into a pattern of negative behavior—yelling, threatening, bribing, or spanking. Focus on the unique qualities of your child and remember to treat her with the same manners and respect you are trying to instill in her. Rainey observed that signing has helped her daughter Emma express her feelings as well as her regret for "toddlerish" behavior. "My daughter signs SAD when she does something she knows is wrong."

Here are some final wise reminders for avoiding toddler temper tantrums:

○ Stick to a routine: schedules provide predictability and comfort for your child.
○ Feed and hydrate toddlers, and let them sleep as needed. (This same piece of advice should be applied to frazzled parents as well.)
○ Realize that temporary disruptions in your routine, such as traveling or the arrival of a guest in your home—or larger disruptions in your family life, such as a new baby, child care situation, or new house—may possibly trigger a tantrum or other negative behavior.

If your child becomes so upset during a temper tantrum that she is fainting or vomiting, it is advisable to consult with your pediatrician, as there may be other health concerns. Additional behaviors that would warrant a conversation with your pediatrician include a child's habitual destruction of property or aggression toward other children.

Lu Hanessian, author of *Let the Baby Drive: Navigating the Road of New Motherhood* (St. Martin's), made this observation about her toddler son: "I notice that the more I give him a say, the more he listens. The more I empathize with his frustrations, the less he tends to hold on to them. The more I focus on the emotion behind the outburst, the shorter his meltdown."

Remember that tantrums are an essential *communication* experience for children. As they begin to separate ever so gradually from their parents, they become passionate about their need to try to solve problems and do things on their own. So the next time your toddler throws a tantrum, remind yourself that her quest for independence at all costs is just another toddler milestone to celebrate, no different than getting a new tooth or riding a tricycle for the first time.

Smile to yourself, take a deep breath, and sing louder.

Daddy stays cool, calm, and collected during Tabitha's tantrum.

BOOKS TO READ

Mother animals cuddle their sleepy babies to sleep in the classic *Time for Bed* (Red Wagon Books) by Mem Fox. The cadence and gently repeating stanzas of the poetry go a long way toward soothing your toddler right into bed. The story is perfect for singing to a tune of your own making. Fox includes many of the animals in the *Toddler Sing & Sign* program, so use her book as a tool for practicing sign language vocabulary as well as snuggling with your child.

DONKEY

Do Donkeys Dance? by Melanie Walsh (Houghton Mifflin)
Little Donkey Close Your Eyes by Margaret Wise Brown (Harper Trophy)
Sylvester and the Magic Pebble by William Steig (Aladdin)
The Little Donkey by Louise Gardner (Autumn Publishing)
Tingalayo by Raffi (Dragonfly Books)

GRAY

Big Yellow Trucks and Diggers by Caterpillar (Chronicle Books)
Baby's Colors by Neil Ricklen (Little Simon)
Huckle Cat's Colors by Richard Scarry (Simon Spotlight)
Kipper's Book of Colors by Mick Inkpen (Red Wagon Books)
A Picnic with Monet by Julie Merberg and Suzanne Bober (Chronicle Books)

EAT/FOOD

Let's Eat! by Andrea Posner (Golden Books)

Do Cows Eat Cake: A Book about What Animals Eat by Michael Dahl (Picture Window Books)

Eat Your Dinner! by Virginia Miller (Candlewick Press)

Who Eats Bananas? by Richard Powell (Treehouse Children's Books Limited)

Baby Food by Margaret Miller (Little Simon)

PLAY

When We Play Together by Nick Butterworth (Little, Brown)

Baby's World: Look at Me I Can Play! by DK Publishing (DK Preschool)

Yippee! Time to Play! by Tina Freeman (Brimax Books)

Miffy at Play: A Flip Book by Dick Bruna (Kodansha America)

Bugs at Play by David A. Carter (Little Simon)

SLEEP

The Going-to-Bed Book by Sandra Boynton (Little Simon)

I Love You As Much by Laura Krauss Melmed (HarperFestival)

Time for Bed by Mem Fox (Red Wagon Books)

Good Night, Sleep Tight by Claire Freedman (Harry N. Abrams)

Good Night, Gorilla by Peggy Rathmann (Putnam Juvenile)

DOWN ON GRANDPA'S FARM

ANIMAL WORDS TO LEARN: **HEN, CAT, SHEEP/LAMB, HORSE**
COLOR WORDS TO LEARN: **ORANGE, BLACK, WHITE, BLUE**
OTHER WORDS TO LEARN: **FRIEND, GIRL, BOY, TRUCK, PRETTY***
WORDS TO REVIEW: **RED, BROWN, DOG, PLAY, BIG, LITTLE*, EYES***

This favorite children's song helps toddlers learn to sing and sign the names of farm animals. It is also a favorite game for practicing the sounds that animals make.

Verse 1:
Down on Grandpa's farm,
There is a LITTLE RED HEN,   *Sign HEN*
Down on Grandpa's farm,
There is a LITTLE RED HEN,   *Sign HEN*
The LITTLE HEN,
She sounds like this: "cluck, cluck"   *Sign HEN on "cluck, cluck"*
The LITTLE HEN,   *Sign HEN*
She sounds like this: "cluck, cluck"   *Sign HEN on "cluck, cluck"*

Chorus:
Oh come, my FRIENDS,   *Sign FRIENDS or clap hands*
Oh come, my FRIENDS,
Oh come to Grandpa's farm.
Oh come, my FRIENDS,
Oh come, my FRIENDS,
Oh come to Grandpa's farm.

---

* These bonus signs are found in the *Toddler Sing & Sign* Dictionary (page 207).

Verse 2:
Down on Grandpa's farm,
There is a LITTLE ORANGE CAT . . .   *Sign CAT*
The LITTLE CAT,   *Sign CAT*
He sounds like this: "meow, meow" . . .   *Sign CAT on "meow, meow"*

Verse 3:
Down on Grandpa's farm,
There is a LITTLE BLACK DOG . . .   *Sign DOG*
The LITTLE DOG,   *Sign DOG*
He sounds like this: "woof, woof" . . .   *Sign DOG on "woof, woof"*

Verse 4:
Down on Grandpa's farm,
There is a wooly WHITE LAMB . . .   *Sign LAMB*
The wooly LAMB,   *Sign LAMB*
He sounds like this: "baah, baah" . . .   *Sign LAMB on "baah, baah"*

Verse 5:
Down on Grandpa's farm,
There is a BIG BROWN HORSE . . .   *Sign HORSE*
The BIG BROWN HORSE,   *Sign HORSE*
He sounds like this: neigh, neigh . . .   *Sign HORSE on "neigh, neigh"*

Verse 6:
Down on Grandpa's farm,
There is a BIG BLUE TRUCK . . .   *Sign TRUCK*
The BIG BLUE TRUCK,   *Sign TRUCK*
It sounds like this: vroom, vroom!   *Sign TRUCK on "vroom, vroom!"*

Verse 7:
Down on Grandpa's farm,
There is a PRETTY young GIRL . . .   *Sign GIRL*
The PRETTY GIRL,   *Sign GIRL*
She sounds like this: let's PLAY . . .   *Sign PLAY*

DOWN ON GRANDPA'S FARM

Traditional / Adapted by Anne Meeker Miller

HEN

Thumb and pointer finger of one hand open and close at mouth like a beak, then tap fingers on palm.

Child may open and close hand or pat closed hand on palm. Child may do only one of these two motions.

CAT

Pull pinched thumb and pointer finger from cheek to show cat's whiskers.

Child may brush cheek with pointer finger or fingertips. Child may perform the sign with two hands on either side of the face.

SHEEP/LAMB

Make cutting motions "shearing the sheep" with *two open fingers* on top of other arm. Move the "shears" up the extended arm.

Child may pat or place fingertips or hand on extended arm.

HORSE

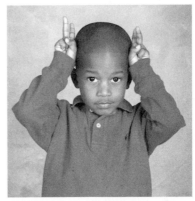

Show the horse's "ears" by placing thumb at temple and bending two closed fingers up and down.

Child may place one or both pointer fingers or cupped hands on either side of head.

ORANGE

Place *closed fist* at chin, and open and close as if "squeezing" a juicy orange.

Child may place or tap fist on chin.

BLACK

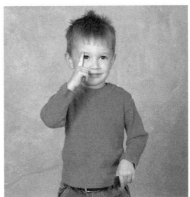

Pull pointer finger across forehead.

Child may touch forehead with pointer finger or fingertips.

WHITE

Open hand in front of chest pulls out to *gathered fingers.*

Child may place or pat chest with hand, or may place fingertips in front of chest without pulling out.

BLUE

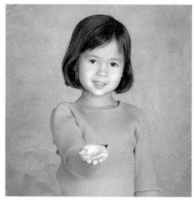

One *closed hand* with thumb against palm twists back and forth at wrist.

Child may move closed hand in a chopping motion.

FRIEND

Curved pointer fingers hook, then hook again in opposite direction.

Child may hook or tap pointer fingers or fingertips together without alternating direction, or simply place one hand on top of the other.

GIRL

Drag thumb down jaw.

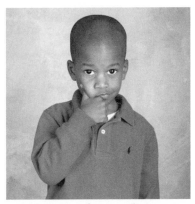

Child may draw fingertips down jaw or press thumb against cheek.

BOY

Gather fingers at forehead as if holding the bill of a ball cap.

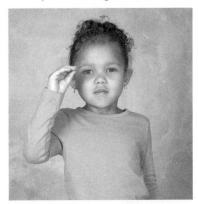

Child may tap fingers or *open hand* on forehead, brow, or cheek.

TRUCK

Hands grasp the large imaginary steering wheel of a truck and pretend to drive.

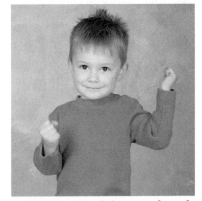

Child may swing whole arms in front of chest without alternating them.

TIPS FOR INTRODUCING
DOWN ON GRANDPA'S FARM

○ Sign the animal names as you make their sounds. Make the motion in time with the animal sound. For instance, when you say, "cluck, cluck," tap your pinched thumb and pointer finger upon your palm two times—one for each "cluck." This will develop your child's ability to segment words by hearing and doing a motion for each syllable.

○ Clap your hands enthusiastically or pat your thighs on the chorus. ("Oh, come my FRIENDS. . . .")

○ You can also sign FRIEND throughout the chorus. Be ready to accept a modified version of this sign from your child, as it requires some coordination to be able to hook pointer fingers and then reverse the gesture. If you are singing this song and your toddler is studying his wiggling fingers or touching them together, praise him for saying FRIEND with his hands.

♪ More Musical Fun with *Down on Grandpa's Farm*

Maizie signs ROOSTER with her mother.

● Make a new version of the "Down on Grandpa's Farm" song for your adventures in the world, such as "Down at Daddy's park there is a bushy, brown squirrel . . ." or "Down at Grandma's store there is a juicy, ORANGE CARROT. . . . The LITTLE GIRL, she EATS like this—crunch, crunch!"

● Sing the song wrong on purpose! Try a version where you sing the animal sound first, and your child can try to guess the animal's name. Your lyrics could be: "Down on Grandpa's farm there is an 'meow, meow, meow' . . . The little critter is a _____." See if your child will say or sign the animal sound when you make the animal sound first.

● Sing about a "Rainbow Farm" and sign the color of the animal instead of the animal name. You can improvise a new lyric, such as "The little SHEEP's the color WHITE, WHITE, WHITE!" However, your child may insist that you make the animal sounds at the "Rainbow Farm" as well.

GAMES AND ACTIVITIES

"Toddler, Toddler, What Do You See?" Book

VOCABULARY PRACTICE: HEN, CAT, DOG, LAMB, HORSE, BOY, GIRL, RED, ORANGE, BLACK, WHITE, BROWN, BLUE, MOMMY*, DADDY*

DEVELOPMENTAL BENEFITS: using pictures to create meaning, book facility, sequencing, fluency

MATERIALS: pictures of animals, construction paper, paper punch, paste, five plastic sheet protectors, yarn

DIRECTIONS: Find pictures of a HEN, CAT, DOG, LAMB, and HORSE, as well as your toddler's MOMMY, DADDY, or other caring adults and family members. An Internet search engine is a great resource for finding animal pictures: go to www.google.com or www.msn.com and click on "Images." Then type the name of the animal you wish to find. You will have many to choose from. Click on the one you like best, and print the image. You can also cut pictures out of magazines for this activity.

Cut pieces of construction paper to fit inside each plastic sheet protector. Paste the pictures of HEN, DOG, LAMB, and HORSE, as well as other caring adults and family members in the center of each piece of construction paper and slide into the plastic sheet protectors. Cut three lengths of yarn approximately six inches long. Make a book of the sheets by tying the pages together loosely, threading one piece of yarn through each of the three holes at the edge of the plastic sheet protectors.

With your child in your lap or by your side, ask, "[child's name], [child's name], what do you see?" Point to the picture of the hen. Wait to see if he will sign or say HEN. Next ask your child to point to the hen. Then say and sign, "I SEE a HEN looking at me." Repeat for the other pages

This is a great story to sing to the tune of "Twinkle, Twinkle, Little Star." Add pages as you learn more animal signs and words. You

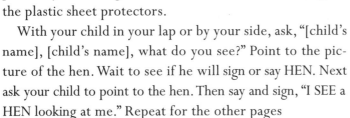

Books are wonderful teaching tools for sign language learning.

---

* These bonus signs are found in the *Toddler Sing & Sign* Dictionary (page 207).

can also add pictures of other important people in your child's life: grandparents, siblings, pets, or caregivers. At the end of the book you can move backward from the last page to the first by saying and pointing: "I see a DADDY, a MOMMY, a GIRL, a HORSE, a LAMB, a DOG, a CAT, and a HEN looking at me!" This activity is a lovely extension of the classic picture book, *Brown Bear, Brown Bear, What Do You See?* by Bill Martin Jr. (see "Books to Read," page 61).

You can also combine color words with the animals if you locate photographs for your book of a RED HEN, BLACK DOG, or any of the other animals in the song.

Sing or read the story slowly and show your child how to sign both the color and the animal word. The music helps the child sign in time with the tune. This is a musical version of an important reading skill called *fluency,* where the child maintains a steady pace and uses inflection as he reads (or sings!).

♪ Barnyard Bustle Play Mat

VOCABULARY PRACTICE: **HEN, CAT, DOG, LAMB, HORSE, GIRL, BOY, RED, ORANGE, BLACK, WHITE, BROWN, BLUE**

DEVELOPMENTAL BENEFITS: purposeful large-motor movement, animal and color identification, following directions, focused listening

MATERIALS: large plastic tablecloth or oilcloth, clear Con-Tact paper, large pictures of animals and colors

DIRECTIONS: Spread the large tablecloth on the floor. Place the animal and color pictures randomly on the tablecloth, and then cover each picture with the clear Con-Tact paper to adhere it to the tablecloth. If you are artistically inclined, you can paint or draw pictures of the animals on your play mat. Cover the drawings and paintings with clear Con-Tact paper to protect them and adhere them to the tablecloth. Your Barnyard Bustle Play Mat is ready to be tested.

Invite your child to come and play Barnyard Bustle. Have your child take off his shoes and socks to make sure that he can move about safely on the play mat without slipping. Tell your child to turn on his "listening ears" because you are going to play a fun game.

While listening to "Down on Grandpa's Farm," help your child to jump, stand, stomp, or sit on the appropriate animal (HEN, CAT, DOG, LAMB,

HORSE) on the play mat when he hears the word in the song. Show him the sign for each animal name and sound as it occurs in the song. See if your child will move to the correct picture on the mat.

You are ready to add more activities to your child's Barnyard Bustle when he is able to move about the play mat easily and find the animals with minimal assistance. Play mat games can be played over and over and in several different ways. As your

Maia and Maizie look for farm animals on the Barnyard Bustle Play Mat.

child masters one way, you can continue to have fun with that version and introduce a new one. He can also follow your spoken and signed direction to: "JUMP on the SHEEP—baa, baa!" "SIT on the HORSE—neeeeiggghh!" "DANCE on the HEN—cluck, cluck!" or "RUN on the DOG—arf, arf!" Invite other family members to play Barnyard Bustle with you. Limit the number of people on the play mat at the same time to two so that it doesn't get too crowded.

Make sure that you state the directions slowly and repeat them as often as your child needs to complete the task. Keep the tasks manageable and fun. Enjoy your Barnyard Bustle play mat and remember that learning is fun. The more fun we have, the more we learn!

♪ Grandpa's Barnyard Box

VOCABULARY PRACTICE: **HEN, CAT, DOG, LAMB, HORSE, GIRL, BOY, RED, ORANGE, BLACK, WHITE, BROWN, BLUE, BIG, LITTLE***

DEVELOPMENTAL BENEFITS: tactile stimulation, color/animal/animal sound identification, size discrimination, imaginary play

MATERIALS: large shoebox; nine plastic lids from a variety of containers (cottage cheese, margarine, yogurt, sour cream, etc.); solid-color and clear Con-Tact paper; pictures of animals; colored paper or markers to color paper; small photograph of your child; child-sized cowboy hat and/or bandana (optional); large jingle bells (optional)

---

* This bonus sign is found in the *Toddler Sing & Sign* Dictionary (page 207).

Maia and Maizie put their animal lids in
Grandpa's Barnyard Box.

DIRECTIONS: To create the Barnyard Box, cover the large shoebox with the solid-color Con-Tact paper and cover the lid separately. Next, cut out circles of solid-color and clear Con-Tact paper to match the size of each plastic lid. Put the solid color on the tops of each lid. Cut the animal pictures to match the size of a lid, place them on the top of the lids, and cover with the clear Con-Tact paper. Cut a large slit on the top of the shoebox lid to match the size of the largest animal lid. Now your animals are ready to visit Grandpa's Barnyard.

Invite your child to come and play with the Barnyard Box. Place the box in front of him, and spread the animal lids (animal side up) all around on both sides of the box to encourage your child to reach for each object. Tell your child that he is a cowboy who works on Grandpa's Farm. It is his job to help Grandpa find the animals on the farm and get them into the Barnyard Box before dark. If you have a cowboy hat and bandana, your child can wear them with this imaginary cowboy play.

While listening to "Down on Grandpa's Farm," help your child drop the lid with the appropriate animal picture (HEN, CAT, DOG, SHEEP, HORSE, DOG) in the box when he hears the word in the song. Sign the word and state the sound that each animal makes as your child drops its picture in the box. Once all of the animal lids are in the box, your child can shake the box as musical accompaniment for the remainder of the song. Place a few large jingle bells inside the box for additional musical fun. *Be certain the bells are too large to fit through an empty cardboard toilet paper roll; this is the test often suggested for determining if an item could be a choking hazard for a small child.*

See if your child can point to the BIG lid and the LITTLE lid. Make the animal sounds, and see if your child can select the lid that matches the animal sound you produce. See if he can produce the animal sounds, too. Last, count the lids, touching each one as you count and say the number aloud.

Once your child is able to find and insert the animal lids when he hears them in the song, you can include a lid with a child's photograph or picture for the "blue-eyed GIRL" or BOY in the song. You can even make additional animal lids and create new verses to the song, too.

Now Grandpa needs your help. Go rustle up those animals!

A SIGN OF SUCCESS

♪ LEARN TO MOVE AND MOVE TO LEARN: ♪ THE VALUE OF ACTIVE PLAY FOR TODDLERS

Get your motor runnin'
Head out on the driveway,
Lookin' for adventure,
And whatever comes our way!
—"BORN TO BE WILD"
BY MARS BONFIRE

My apologies to the rock band Steppenwolf for slightly altering the lyrics of their 1968 pop classic "Born to Be Wild." I doubt the song's composer realized he had created an anthem for toddlers everywhere when he wrote this tune.

Having hit "pay dirt" with the gift of locomotion made possible through typical development, toddlers not only learn to coordinate their large muscle movements to walk, but can now feed and dress themselves with assistance and start to contemplate mastery of toilet training.

There are two main types of motor motion: *gross-motor* and *fine-motor*. Gross-motor development refers to large-muscle movement of arms, legs, and torso; fine-motor development refers to the actions of the muscles that control smaller, more isolated movements of the fingers and hands. Gross-motor development usually occurs before fine-motor, and progresses from the child's head to his toes.

It is important to give children opportunities to move and explore so that they can develop confidence in their self-help and problem-solving abilities. Let him learn by doing, exploring the world with his senses. Let him pour cups of water into a bucket, paint a picture with pudding, hide toys in the sandbox, and smell the cinnamon and nutmeg as you make muffins.

Movement and play are essential experiences for toddlers. According to Dr. Marvalene Moore, Professor of Music Education at the University of Kentucky, movement is the life line to the young child's musical being—their imagination, understanding, performance, and creativity. Says Moore: "For the young child, to move is to be and to be is to move." Lynn Kleiner, early childhood music educator and director of the Music Rhapsody program, has found that children best understand concepts when they are physically experienced. For example, to demonstrate the concept of "high," she sings with a high voice and shows the children how to reach with their arms high above their heads. Then, in contrast, she demonstrates "low" by using appropriate "low" motions and singing pitches. According to Kleiner, "This demonstration of the meaning of the words not only helps a toddler master new vocabulary, but also develops a conceptual understanding of complex ideas, as well as coordination, listening skills, and the ability to sing in tune."

Movement and play are likewise essential experiences. Laura Murphy, a parenting specialist and founder of the Real Families educational program, notes that exploration and physical activity are crucial for development of both mind and body. According to Murphy, "The multitude of neural fibers in a toddler's brain are working hard to form and connect—and to 'build the brain' they will use their entire life to reason, problem solve and relate to others." Murphy challenges parents to ignore the clutter of toys and materials that make active and creative play possible. Instead, celebrate the value of immersing children in discovery and imagination.

Toddler Sing & Sign is perfectly suited for toddlers who are eager to move and play as they learn. The songs engage children in both fine- and gross-motor movement as they learn new signs for animals, actions, colors, and other key words used in communication. They use their bodies as well as their fingers to dance, sing, and sign their animal tunes.

Sign language is also a "picture language" in its use of gestures to represent words or ideas. Usually the sign approximates, or looks like, the word it represents; the CRAWDAD sign uses two fingers to form this animal's claws, and the BABY sign is performed by rocking an imaginary baby in your arms. Signs give your child the ability to understand and communicate abstract ideas that cannot be seen, such as LOVE or AFRAID, by representing them with a gesture.

Toddler Sing & Sign is perfectly suited for toddlers who are eager to move and play as they learn. The songs engage children in both fine- and gross-motor movement as they learn new signs for animals, actions, colors, and other key words used in communication.

Using a sign to represent an object, idea, or concept is called *iconic learning* and is actually a prerequisite to learning to read. The signed word is the icon, or symbol, the toddler uses to represent new learning. This icon eventually becomes the printed picture of the preschooler and the written word of the kindergartner. All young children are on a continuum of child development as they master the art of interpreting images that represent language.

For toddlers, movement is the method best suited for them to "show what they know."

Sign language incorporates movement play to support the comprehension of new concepts such as big and little, fast and slow. For instance, the "great BIG grizzly BEAR" is sung and signed by extending your arms over your head to show how very tall the bear must be. The child uses movement to make the connection between his image of the big bear described in the ballad and his concrete manner of estimating the bear's size with sign language.

In addition, *Toddler Sing & Sign* advocates free play in equal measure with sign language and music. The notion that rich and interesting play materials do not need to be purchased from a toy store is an important principle of this program. Laundry baskets make wonderful pretend cars or beds for imaginary baby animals. Playing the pots-and-pans "drum set" in the kitchen is a perfect musical accompaniment to the songs on the *Toddler Sing & Sign* CD.

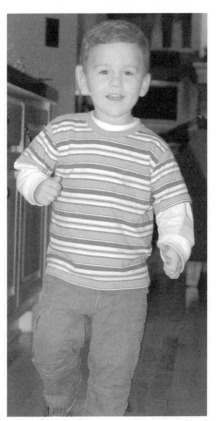

A recently published report from the American Academy of Pediatrics prescribed spontaneous free play for a nation prone to overscheduling and overstressing our children. With the overwhelming number of videos and classes available that pledge to make babies and toddlers smarter, it is easy to neglect quality time spent on the floor building with blocks, playing on the swings and slide at the park, or stealing some snuggle time on the couch after breakfast. Hopefully the academy's report will give parents permission to give up the urge to "superparent" in favor of allowing children the luxury of "un-*adult*-erated" play with no expectation of their activity other than fun.

You have my blessing to set this book down immediately if you promise to load your toddler into the wagon with a water bottle and a tasty snack and take him to play at the park. *Toddler Sing & Sign* will still be here when you return!

Children learn important skills through movement exploration and free play.

BOOKS TO READ

"Old MacDonald" is at the top of my list of tunes children should know by heart by the time they go to preschool. The song is not only playful, but it's also wonderful for helping children remember a sequence of animals and gives toddlers the chance to practice their animal sounds. Amy Schwartz makes learning this classic song easy and fun with her picture-book rendition of *Old MacDonald* (Scholastic). She manages a perfect balance of realistic farm action and whimsical animal antics. Old MacDonald even has a "song" on his farm—" . . . and on his farm he had a song . . . with a tra la la here and a tra la la there."

HEN

Big Fat Hen by Keith Baker (Red Wagon Books)

Hen and Chick by Helen Montardre (Two-Can)

Hen's Pens by Phil Roxbee Cox and Jenny Tyler (Usborne)

Rosie's Walk by Pat Hutchins (Aladdin)

The Little Red Hen by Ronne Randall (Ladybird Books)

CAT

A Cat and a Dog by Claire Masurel and Bob Kolar (North-South)

I Love Cats by Barney Saltzberg (Candlewick Press)

Mama Cat Has Three Kittens by Denise Fleming (Owlet Paperbacks)

Ten Cats Have Hats by Jean Marzollo (Cartwheel Books)

Pat the Cat by Edith Kunhardt Davis (Golden Books)

LAMB

Lamb by Deni Bown (Dorling Kindersley)

Mary Had a Little Lamb by Sarah Josepha Hale and Bruce McMillan (Scholastic)

Sheep in a Jeep by Nancy Shaw (Houghton Mifflin)

Sheep in a Shop by Nancy Shaw (Houghton Mifflin)

The Lamb and the Butterfly by Arnold Sundgaard and Eric Carle (Orchard Books)

HORSE

All the Pretty Little Horses by Linda Saport (Clarion Books)

Clarene Goes out West and Meets a Purple Horse by Jean Ekman Adams (Rising Moon Books)

My Little Rocking Horse Lullabies by Caroline Davis (Little Simon)

Pocket Pony by Pam Adams (Child's Play International)

The Wild Little Horse by Rita Gray (Dutton Juvenile)

ORANGE

Color Zoo Board Book by Lois Ehlert (HarperFestival)

My Many Colored Days by Dr. Seuss (Knopf Books for Young Readers)

Orange, Pear, Apple, Bear by Emily Gravett (Macmillan Children's Books)

Planting a Rainbow by Lois Ehlert (Voyager Books)

Why is an Orange Called an Orange? By Cobi Ladner (McArthur and Company)

BLACK

Baby Animals Black and White by Phyllis Limbacher Tildes (Charlesbridge)

Black Dog Gets Dressed by Lizi Boyd (Candlewick Press)

Black on White by Tana Hoban (Greenwillow Books)

Black Cat, White Moon by Nina Alexander (GT Publishing)

Old Black Fly by Jim Aylesworth (Henry Holt)

WHITE

Little White Dogs Can't Jump by Bruce Whatley (HarperCollins)

Little White Duck by Bernard Zaritzky and Joan Paley (Little, Brown Young Readers)

Max and Ruby's Snowy Day by Rosemary Wells (Grosset and Dunlap)

The Little White Dog by Laura Godwin (Hyperion)

White Rabbit's Color Book by Alan Baker (Kingfisher)

BLUE

A Boy and His Bunny by Sean Bryan (Arcade)

Blue Hat, Green Hat by Sandra Boynton (Little Sim on)

Dog Blue by Polly Dunbar (Candlewick Press)

Is It Red? Is It Yellow? Is It Blue? by Tana Hoban (Greenwillow Books)

The Deep Blue Sea: A Book of Colors by Audrey Wood (Blue Sky Press)

FRIEND

A Rainbow of Friends by P. K. Hallinan (Ideals Children's Books)

Baby's Animal Friends by Phoebe Dunn (Random House Books for Young Readers)

Dumpy's Friends on the Farm by Julie Andrews Edwards and Emma Walton Hamilton (Hyperion)

My Best Friend by Pam Huizenga (Avalon Lane)

Where Is My Friend? by Marcus Pfister (North-South)

GIRL

I Want to Be a Cowgirl by Jeanne Willis (Henry Holt)

Love from My Heart to a Precious Girl by Heidi Weimer (Candy Cane Press)

Mary Wore Her Red Dress and Henry Wore His Green Sneakers by Merle Peek (Clarion Books)

Motown: My Girl—Book #1 by Charles R. Smith (Jump at the Sun)

When I'm a Big Sister by Bruce Lansky (Meadowbrook)

BOY

I Love You, Stinky Face by Lisa McCourt (Scholastic)

Little Boy Blue (The Mother Goose Collection) by Rosemary Wells (Walker Books)

Love from My Heart to a Snuggly Cuddly Little Boy: Parent Love Letters by Heidi Weimer (Candy Cane Press)

The Gingerbread Boy by Paul Galdone (Clarion Books)

The Noisy Way to Bed by Ian Whybrow (Arthur A. Levine Books)

TRUCK

A Truck Goes Rattley-Bumpa by Jonathan London and Denis Roche (Henry Holt)

Go, Go, Trucks! by Simon Hart (Price Stern Sloan)

My Big Truck Book by Roger Priddy (Priddy Books)

My Truck Is Stuck by Kevin Lewis (Hyperion)

The Happy Man and His Dump Truck by Tibor Gergely (Golden Books)

I'M A TURTLE

ANIMAL WORD TO LEARN: **TURTLE**
COLOR WORD TO LEARN: **GREEN**
OTHER WORDS TO LEARN: **SLOW, FAST, ALL DONE, HIDE**
WORDS TO REVIEW: **GLAD/HAPPY, MUSIC/SONG, LOOK**

This song was written in honor of my friend Carter, who wanted to be a turtle so much that he became one in his imagination for several weeks straight. He is back to being a boy named Carter now. However, whether a turtle or a little boy, he loves to sing his turtle song to anyone who will listen.

The delightful music and poetry of the Kansan Charles Golladay capture the essence of "turtle-ness" we were striving for in Toddler Sing & Sign. The Warner Brothers recording artist Jim "Mr. Stinky Feet" Cosgrove brought our singing turtle to life with his rich baritone voice and toddler sense of humor.

Left, right, left, right,	*Sway to the beat*
You think I'm SLOW,	*Sign SLOW*
And of course you're right!	
I'm a TURTLE,	*Sign TURTLE*
I'm a TURTLE.	*Sign TURTLE*
Others pass me by with their hectic [FAST] pace,	*Sign FAST*
But SLOW and steady always wins the race,	*Sign SLOW*
I'm a TURTLE,	*Sign TURTLE*
I'm a TURTLE.	*Sign TURTLE*
I may be SLOW but I'm doing fine,	*Sign SLOW*
I may take my time but I'm not behind,	
You hurry, hurry, hurry,	*Sign FAST*

To get home on time [FAST],	*Sign FAST*
All I need to do is STOP,	*Sign STOP*
And I am safe in mine,	
I'm a TURTLE,	*Sign TURTLE*
I'm a TURTLE.	*Sign TURTLE*
Left, right, left, right,	*Sway to the beat*
I'll make it where I'm going,	
If it takes all night,	
I'm a TURTLE,	*Sign TURTLE*
I'm a TURTLE.	*Sign TURTLE*
If it starts to rain, I will say: "Oh well,"	*Shrug shoulders*
It's always dry here inside my shell [HIDE],	*Sign HIDE*
I'm a TURTLE,	*Sign TURTLE*
I'm a TURTLE.	*Sign TURTLE*
Life is good and all TURTLES know,	*Sign TURTLE*
There really is no reason to rush to and fro [FAST],	*Sign FAST*
I like to SEE the scenery every where I go,	*Sign SEE*
Often you're much better if you take things SLOW,	*Sign SLOW*
Like a TURTLE,	*Sign TURTLE*
And I'm a TURTLE.	*Sign TURTLE*
Left, right, left, right	*Sway to the beat*
You ask me if I'm finished [ALL DONE],	*Sign ALL DONE*
And I'll say, "Not quite,"	*Shake head: "No!"*
I'm a TURTLE,	*Sign TURTLE*
I'm a TURTLE.	*Sign TURTLE*
I hope that you have enjoyed my SONG,	*Sign SONG*
Please don't sing it FASTER,	*Sign FAST*
That would just be wrong,	
For a TURTLE,	*Sign TURTLE*
And I'm a TURTLE.	*Sign TURTLE*

I have to go,
Because my SONG is through [ALL DONE],   *Sign SONG and ALL DONE*
It makes me HAPPY spending time with you,   *Sign HAPPY*
I like to stick around but you know it's true,
Even a TURTLE has got things to do,   *Sign TURTLE*
And I'm a TURTLE,   *Sign TURTLE*
I'm a TURTLE,   *Sign TURTLE*
I'm a TURTLE.   *Sign TURTLE*

Jim "Mr. Stinky Feet" Cosgrove
and our "turtle" friend, Carter

I'M A TURTLE

TURTLE

Place a *cupped hand* over *closed fist* and wiggle thumb as if a turtle's "head" is peeking from his "shell."

Child will likely place one hand on top of the other, or place hand on arm.

GREEN

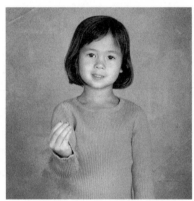

Thumb and pointer finger of one hand twists back and forth.

Child may shake pointer finger or whole hand.

SLOW

Move *open hand* up other arm from hand to elbow in slow motion.

Child may pat hand on arm without performing the slow upward motion.

FAST

Cupped hands close as thumbs pop up quickly.

Child may move *closed fists* up.

ALL DONE

Hold *open hands* in front of you with palms toward your chest. Flip hands to palms facing down.

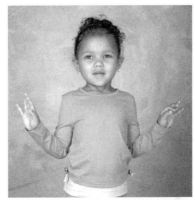

Child may throw hands up toward shoulders.

HIDE

Closed fist of one hand with thumb extended "hides" under other *cupped hand*.

Child may place one hand over the other, similar to her TURTLE sign.

TIPS FOR INTRODUCING
I'M A TURTLE

○ Start simply by signing the word TURTLE as you hear it in the story. TURTLE is a fun sign to perform, and includes hand shapes that are simple for toddlers to do.

○ There are repeating portions of the song that include the TURTLE sign as you sing, "I'm a TURTLE" (the chorus). There are portions of the song that tell a different little part of the story in between each repetition of the chorus (the verses). Your toddler will begin to anticipate when the chorus will return and be ready with his TURTLE sign. This is a marvelous demonstration of his emerging musical skills: he can detect the pattern and form in the song.

○ Allow your child to enjoy both the turtle story and the different quality of the singer's voice. She is used to hearing a woman's voice singing on the *Toddler Sing & Sign* CD, and this new timbre of a man's singing voice will be an interesting change for her.

○ SINGING and SONG are signed by using the same gesture used for signing MUSIC.

Adelina and her mother march "left, right" as they sing "I'm a Turtle" to transition from outdoor play to lunchtime.

♪ More Musical Fun with *I'm a Turtle*

● "I'm a Turtle" is a great song to walk or dance to. With the "left, right, left, right" refrain, it reminds the listener of a marching chant an army might use to keep its soldiers stepping in time. You can do some marching, walking, or dancing to the beat at your house.

● Once you have listened to the "I'm a Turtle" song many times, try singing just the first verse without the CD: "Left, right, left, right, you think I'm SLOW and of course you're right! I'm a TURTLE!" Sing the lyrics slowly in an exaggerated fashion. Move your feet slowly as you sing. Perhaps your child will imitate your motions. Most certainly she will laugh out loud! Then try singing verses about other animals. For example, " . . . you think I'm FAST and of course you're right! I'm a HORSEY!" Sing the lyrics quickly and add a gallop or trot to your singing. Let your child choose animals and decide whether she wants them to move fast or slow.

- Sing the "I'm a Turtle" song to transition your child from one activity to another. It is so engaging and fun that toddlers won't mind that they are marching from playtime to naptime or from grandmother's house to their car seat. Simply sing with gusto as you and your toddler move!

GAMES AND ACTIVITIES

♪ "Silly Turtle" Locomotion Game

VOCABULARY PRACTICE: **TURTLE, SLOW, FAST, STOP, LOVE**

DEVELOPMENTAL BENEFITS: focused listening and looking, following simple directions, awareness of slow and fast, motor planning

MATERIALS: none needed

Gianni and his mother travel to their own "turtle beat."

DIRECTIONS: this silly performance of the "I'm a Turtle" song will help your child experience the abstract concepts of fast and slow. Take her hand and begin to walk as you sing the song unaccompanied by the music CD. You don't need to memorize all of the lyrics; the first verse will work perfectly ("Left, right, left, right, you think I'm SLOW and of course you're right! I'm a TURTLE, I'm a TURTLE"—then repeat!).

You can travel around the house, take a walk to the mailbox, or travel around your backyard. Ask your child if she would like to play the "Silly Turtle" game. She can choose to be a fast turtle or a slow turtle. If she chooses to be FAST, sing the song and walk very quickly. After you sing the chorus ("I'm a TURTLE, I'm a TURTLE"), sing STOP and stand in place. Ask your child again what kind of turtle she would like to be: SLOW or FAST? Repeat the game until she is ready to STOP.

♪ Turtle Obstacle Course

VOCABULARY PRACTICE: **TURTLE, GREEN, SLOW, FAST, HIDE, ALL DONE**

DEVELOPMENTAL BENEFITS: purposeful large-motor movement; sensory stimulation; language concepts such as slow/fast and positional words like under/over/around/through/on; space and depth perception; balance

MATERIALS: throw pillow, belt or long scarf, two blankets, table and chairs, cushions from couch or pillows from bed, three or four small toys, green stocking cap (optional)

DIRECTIONS: Invite your child to help you set up an obstacle course. Take four chairs from the table and set them up on the other side of the room. Create a tunnel with the chairs by lining up two across from another set of two so that they are about one foot away from each other. Arrange the chairs with either the backsides or seat sides of the chairs inside of the tunnel, depending on whether your toddler wants a tunnel that is short or tall, wide or narrow. Put a small blanket over the chairs to create the tunnel. Your child will love crawling through it.

After you make the tunnel, line the small toys in a row about ten inches apart for your child to step over when she is on the course. Next, set couch cushions or bed pillows on the ground for your child to crawl around and over as he explores the course. Cover your kitchen table with a large blanket so that it can become a burrow for your turtle child. At the end of the course, your child will enjoy hiding in her burrow.

Gianni loves his pillow "turtle shell."

Now it is time for your child to put on her turtle shell. Have her get into a crawling position, place a small throw pillow on her back, and gently secure it with a belt or long scarf. *Supervise your child while she is wearing the belt or scarf and put it away when not in use.* An alternative is to have your child wear a large shirt and tuck the throw pillow into her shirt so that the "shell" is on her back. If you have a green stocking cap, she can put it on to look the part of a turtle ready for the course.

If you are up to the challenge, model the steps of the obstacle course for your child. Emphasize the language concepts: *through* the tunnel, *over* the toys, *around/on* the cushions, *under* the table. Play the "I'm a Turtle" song from the CD, and have fun exploring the course. Encourage your child to move FAST and SLOW. When the song is ALL DONE, ask if she would like to do it again. Turtle children have amazing endurance.

♪ Hide the Turtle

VOCABULARY PRACTICE: TURTLE, GREEN, SLOW, FAST, HIDE, ALL DONE

DEVELOPMENTAL BENEFITS: hand-eye coordination, large-motor skills (bending over, stooping, squatting), problem solving

MATERIALS: large plastic bowl or bucket; green toy turtle, or several pictures of turtles covered in clear Con-Tact paper

Isaac discovers the turtle hiding under the pot!

DIRECTIONS: Hide the Turtle is a simple toddler version of the German children's game *Topfschlagen,* or "Hit the Pot." In Germany, young children play this game at birthday parties. A present is placed under a pot and hidden in the room while a child covers his eyes. The child then takes a wooden spoon and hits the ground as he crawls around in search of the pot. When he finds the pot, he gets to keep the present. Then someone else gets to take a turn.

In Hide the Turtle, you will show your child your bowl or bucket and your green toy turtle. Sign TURTLE and GREEN and show him how you will HIDE the turtle under the bowl. Model how to close and cover your eyes by placing your hands over your eyes and then putting your head down (either on the floor or on a couch or chair). Have your child see if she can close and cover her eyes, too. You are being just like the turtle when he hides in his shell.

Have your child close and cover her eyes while you HIDE the bowl (with the turtle) somewhere in the room. Tell your child that you are "ready" and turn on the "I'm a Turtle" song. Help your child find the bowl. You can walk, dance, or crawl as you hunt. When you find the bowl, stop the music and sign TURTLE. With a puzzled look on your face, ask your child where the turtle is. State that it must be hiding and tell her to try to find it. Celebrate when your child lifts the bowl and finds the turtle. Congratulate her and say, "Let's play again!"

Now it is time for your child to find the turtle all by herself. All turtle catchers like being independent while they hunt. Have your child close her eyes. Pick a new spot for the bowl, say that you are ready, and start the music once again. Your turtle catcher will probably return to the first location. Encourage her to keep looking. When she finds the bowl, stop the music and continue by encouraging her to find the TURTLE as stated before. See if your turtle catcher can move SLOWLY while she hunts. See if she can move FAST, too. When the song is over, sign ALL DONE and ask your child if she wants to play again.

A variation on this game is to have several pictures of turtles on different-colored paper. Hide one of the turtle pictures instead of the green toy turtle under the bowl. When your child finds it, she can keep the picture. Have a bag or bucket for her to use to carry her turtles. She can carry the bag with her as she plays the game. At the end of the song, you can examine her catch. Count the turtles and talk about the colors. In addition, you can "dress up" your turtles by adding glitter to the pictures before you cover them with clear Con-Tact paper. Children love finding treasures.

A SIGN OF SUCCESS

♪ THE MARRIAGE OF SONG AND SIGN: A PERFECT UNION ♪ FOR TODDLER LANGUAGE AND LEARNING

> Music is the one art we all have inside. . . . All of us have had the experience of hearing a tune from childhood and having that melody evoke a memory or a feeling. The music we hear early on tends to stay with us all our lives.
> —FRED ROGERS, *The World According To Mister Rogers*

Jennifer began singing to her daughter Maizie the day she was born. Now that Maizie is a toddler, her mother continues to sing songs to her throughout the day, making up verses that include Maizie's name and improvising tunes that include her adored butterflies. There are tunes for Maizie's daily routine from breakfast until bedtime: songs for meals, diaper changes, bath time, and transitioning from home to the store or a friend's house. Those songs that are an integral part of Maizie's day serve to calm her when she is upset and help capture her attention when she is distracted.

Music is especially helpful during car trips; Jennifer sings or turns on a CD and Maizie is "instantly transported to a happy place." Music provides an emotional connection to the activity at hand. Jennifer, a teacher, observed that same positive connection with students in her preschool classroom. The children were naturally motivated to learn and express, because they found the music to be irresistible.

Sarah, the mother of two-year-old Ethan, said it best: "I started the program because I wanted my son to learn to communicate with us before he could speak. However, I continued because the music really 'spoke' to him, and his musical expression has meant as much to me as the signs he used before he could talk to tell me what he wanted and needed."

Parents often report to me that their infant or toddler "really likes music!" The fact of the matter is that I have never met a little child who didn't like music. However, children are even more musically sophisticated than we give them credit for.

○ Sandra E. Trehub, professor of psychology at the University of Toronto at Mississauga, found that infants and adults process music in like fashion. In the earliest months of a child's life, an infant understands that a melody stays the same even if the starting pitch is shifted up or down. The same is true if the tempo (or speed) of a melody is altered; they perceive both performances as being the same melody.

○ Babies often prefer their mother's singing voice to her speaking voice. Her singing voice is calming to them. Researchers at the University of Western Sydney concurred. The gentle singing and stroking provided to infants in the intensive care unit helped to calm and comfort sick babies, moderating their levels of irritability and crying, while sick babies who did not receive the singing sessions did not cope as well with hospitalization and spent more time and energy crying and fussing.

○ Music and language have much in common. Both require a listener to interpret what they hear and find meaning from the order and pattern of sounds. According to one dictionary, music is a product that results from the artful arrangement of sounds in patterns that create a pleasing effect. Many people consider music to be a language in and of itself—a type of nonverbal communication that is unique and specific. A talented speaker is skillful in ordering words in a manner that is informative or persuasive. Both musical notes and spoken words can be arranged with the purpose of stimulating the imagination or drawing out our emotions and intellect.

How does a toddler express herself musically? She will begin to babble and hum. She may play with her voice in a variety of ways that include slides, high- and low-pitched sounds, and jabbering "conversations," where she takes turns "talking" with another caring person. She claps her hands, dances, walks, runs, or kicks her legs in appreciation of a song she likes. She may also become more attentive to the source of the music—a person, CD player, or television—and look to see where the music is coming from.

Toddler Sing & Sign uses music in an appealing way to help children learn and practice new signs. The songs provide the built-in repetition necessary for mastering sign language skills. In addition, the song material—from the red rooster in the kitchen to the duck who sails a ship—serves as a theme for a host of games and activities families can enjoy that provide multiple developmental benefits for young children.

But what about the music itself? Even without the benefit of sign language, music has the power to foster language skills!

○ **Attentive listening is an essential skill for language learning as your toddler begins to associate the sounds she hears with specific meaning.** Music also demands active participation; a network of neural connections is fired when your child listens to the tones and words of a simple song, utilizing several regions of the brain.

○ **She can name objects and begin to express her understanding of concepts such as stop and go, fast and slow, sound and silence.** This process is enhanced when she is hearing songs that help her directly experience these ideas. For example, "All Around the Kitchen" includes directions for "STOP like this," and your toddler responds to the direction she hears.

○ **She is recognizing familiar items and experiences from memory and recalling them by name. She is also categorizing, organizing, and sequencing things.** "Down on Grandpa's Farm" includes animals within a category: they all live on a farm. There is a predictable sequence of animals in this song, as each animal name and sound is performed and then followed by the repeating chorus ("Oh come, my FRIENDS . . ."). Children respond to this type of musical structure and predictability. It is as comforting for a toddler and preschooler as a lullaby is to a brand-new baby.

○ **Your toddler's vocal tract continues to mature, making possible the speech sounds necessary for her to articulate words.** Singing and vocal exploration make possible greater coordination and flexibility of the vocal chords. Her skill at manipulating her mouth, teeth, tongue, and lips is improved as she learns to sing the words of her favorite songs.

Dr. Alice Ann Darrow is a professor of music at Florida State University and a music therapist specializing in music for children and adults with hearing impairments. Darrow believes that babies and toddlers innately respond to the sound of music. Music, then, is a valuable tool to partner with signs and gestures—the first language of all young children. As Darrow says, "Such experiences can pave the way for early skill development in: attending, thinking, listening, creating, speaking, and even reading. *Toddler Sing & Sign* gives teachers and parents an appropriate structure for presenting music and signs to their students and children."

And what of the "Mozart effect," a belief that listening to classical music can make young children smarter? This claim was based in large part on findings that for a short period of time after listening to classical music, study participants scored higher on very specific tasks having to do with ordering things in time

> Music and language have much in common. Both require a listener to interpret what they hear and find meaning from the order and pattern of sounds.

as well as mental imagery tasks. This finding promoted the selection of classical music as the genre of choice for young children's listening enjoyment.

We now believe that while music benefits children in a variety of ways, there isn't necessarily a relationship between intelligence and a child's music listening routine. Similarly, children do not become smarter by watching educational videos. Children blossom through their interactions with other caring people in their lives.

Jonann, the mother of an infant and a toddler, credits *Toddler Sing & Sign* for helping her firstborn engage socially with her and her husband as well as others. She also believes it helped her daughter overcome any verbal frustration she had while learning to talk. Now at two, Jonann's daughter sings to her little brother, requests her "Miller" music in the car, and is still interested in learning new signs that she can speak as well as sing. According to Jonann, "*Toddler Sing & Sign* will have a profound impact on my child in the years to come."

Music is magical. It affixes concepts and ideas in a structured fashion into the readily accessible regions of a child's brain. It enhances the bond between you and your child as you communicate using a special "love language" of song and musical play. It provides a powerful medium for new learning in a way that is fun and rewarding for your toddler.

Now that is a song worth singing!

> Singing and vocal exploration make possible greater coordination and flexibility of the vocal chords. A child's skill at manipulating her mouth, teeth, tongue, and lips is improved as she learns to sing the words of her favorite songs.

Older siblings are wonderful sign language teachers for their younger brothers or sisters.

BOOKS TO READ

Charles Turner creates a magical place in his picture book *The Turtle and the Moon* (Dutton Children's Books), where a lonely turtle and the moon can be the best of friends. The story provides plenty of opportunities to practice key vocabulary words used in daily life with toddlers, including SLEEP, PLAY, and RUN. The turtle and the moon HIDE from each other as little by little they become acquainted. Friendship is a gift that comes in many forms, and Turner's wonderful turtle book doesn't hide from this important truth.

TURTLE

Box Turtle at Long Pond by William T. George (Greenwillow Books)

Pond by Lizi Boyd (Chronicle Books)

Tillie Turtle by Annie Kubler (Child's Play International)

Tiny Turtles by Wendy McLean (Book Company Publishing)

Turtle Splash! Countdown at the Pond by Cathryn Falwell (Greenwillow Books)

GREEN

Green: A Touchy Feely First Words Color Book by Melanie Gerth and James Diaz (Piggy Toes Press)

Where Is the Green Sheep? by Mem Fox and Judy Horacek (Harcourt Children's Books

Little Green Tow Truck by Ken Wilson-Max (Cartwheel Books)

Red, Stop! Green, Go! An Interactive Book of Colors by P. D. Eastman (Random House Books for Young Readers)

Red Light, Green Light by Anastasia Suen (Gulliver Books)

SLOW

Dinosaur Roar! by Henrietta Strickland and Paul Strickland (Dutton Juvenile)

Faster, Faster! Nice and Slow! by Nick Sharratt and Sue Heap (Puffin Books)

Mr. Slow by Roger Hargreaves (Price Stern Sloan)

Miss Spider's New Car by David Kirk (Scholastic)

Slow Animals by Dana Simson (Walker Books)

FAST

Bertie and Small and the Fast Bike by Vanessa Cabban (Candlewick Press)

Fast and Faster! by Alan Rubin (Yellow Umbrella Books)

Fast and Slow by Sue Barraclough (Raintree)

Fast and Slow: An Animal Opposites Book by Lisa Bullard (Capstone Press)

Zoom! by Sarah Garland (Frances Lincoln)

ALL DONE

Big Road Machines by Caterpillar (Chronicle Books)

Dishes All Done by Lucia Monfried and Jon Agee (Dutton Children's Books)

Finish the Story, Dad by Nicola Smee (Walker Books)

The Very Hungry Caterpillar by Eric Carle (Philomel)

Yum, Yum, All Done by Jerry Smath (Grosset and Dunap)

HIDE

Five Little Monkeys Play Hide-and-Seek by Eileen Christelow (Clarion Books)

Hide-and-Seek by Janet Morgan Stoeke (Dutton Juvenile)

Hide and Snake by Keith Baker (Voyager Books)

Washington Plays Hide-and-Seek by Dominique Jolin (Dominique)

We Hide, You Seek by Jose Aruego (HarperTrophy)

THE ANIMAL FAIR

ANIMAL WORDS TO LEARN: **ANIMAL, BIRD, BABOON/MONKEY,
ELEPHANT, HIPPO, GIRAFFE, MOOSE, ZEBRA**
OTHER WORD TO LEARN: **WHAT?**
BONUS WORDS: **KNEES*, SNEEZE*, TRAIN***
WORDS TO REVIEW: **HAIR*; MUSIC/SONG, BLUE**

Minstrel shows were popular in the late 1800s. Dan Emmett was a minstrel performer and musician who realized his boyhood dream by joining the circus and performing his music for circus audiences. These early minstrel performances in circus venues may have been the inspiration for the lyrics of "The Animal Fair."

I went to the ANIMAL Fair,   *Sign ANIMAL*
The BIRDS and the beasts were there.   *Sign BIRD*
The big BABOON, by the light of the moon, *Sign MONKEY*
Was combing his auburn HAIR.   *Pretend to comb HAIR or sign HAIR*
The MONKEY, he had spunk!   *Sign MONKEY*
He tickled the ELEPHANT's trunk.   *Sign ELEPHANT*
The ELEPHANT SNEEZED,   *Sign ELEPHANT*
And fell on his KNEES,   *Touch knees*
So WHAT became   *Sign WHAT?*
Of the MONK?   *Sign MONKEY*

I went to the ANIMAL Fair,   *Sign ANIMAL*
The giant GIRAFFE was there.   *Sign GIRAFFE*
The HIPPO got loose,   *Sign HIPPO*
And DANCED with the MOOSE,   *Sign MOOSE*
The two were a jolly [HAPPY] pair!   *Dance or sign HAPPY*

---

* These bonus signs are found in the *Toddler Sing & Sign* Dictionary (page 207).

The ZEBRA joined the crew,   *Sign ZEBRA*
And DANCED 'til his stripes turned BLUE. *Sign BLUE*
The evening wore on,
(And so does this SONG)   *Sign SONG*
But WHAT became   *Sign WHAT?*
Of the MONK?   *Sign MONKEY*

THE ANIMAL FAIR

I   went to the   a - ni - mal   fair.———— The
went to the   a - ni - mal   fair.———— The

birds and the beasts were   there.———The   big—— ba - boon by the
gi - ant gi - raffe was   there.———The   hip - po got loose—— and

light   of   the moon   was   com - bing his   au - burn
danced with   the moose.   The   two were   a   jol - ly

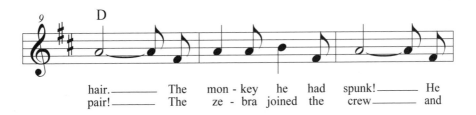

hair.———— The   mon - key   he   had   spunk!———— He
pair!———— The   ze - bra joined the   crew———— and

Traditional / Adapted by Anne Meeker Miller

tick - led the e - le-phant's trunk.— The e - le - phant sneezed and
danced 'til his stripes— turned blue.— The eve-ning wore on (and

fell on his knees. So what be - came of the monk? The monk? The
so does this song) But what be - came of the

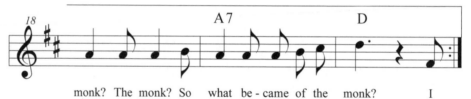

monk? The monk? So what be - came of the monk? I

monk? The monk? The monk? The monk? The monk? The monk? The

monk? The monk? So what be - came of the monk?

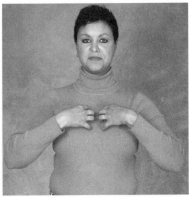

ANIMAL

Show breathing motion of animals by resting open *cupped hands* on chest and rocking them back and forth.

Child may pat tummy or sides. Her ANIMAL sign may look like her BEAR sign.

BIRD

Thumb and pointer finger of one hand open and close at mouth in imitation of bird.

Child may touch mouth with pointer finger, or open and close hand to imitate bird's "beak."

BABOON/ MONKEY

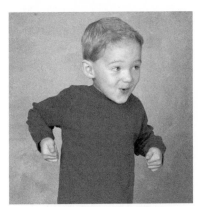

Cupped hands scratch sides in monkey fashion.

Child may tap sides and add "hoo-hoo" monkey sounds.

ELEPHANT

Place back of *closed hand* on nose and move forward and down in shape of an elephant's trunk.

Child may swing extended arm in front of body without touching nose.

HIPPO

Extend thumbs and little fingers of *closed fists*. Place one hand on top of the other and open and close the hippo's "mouth."

Child may clap hands with (or without) one hand on top of the other to form the hippo's "mouth."

GIRAFFE

Cupped hand extends up from neck to above head.

Child may touch or pat neck or point up to show the giraffe's long neck.

MOOSE

Place thumbs of both *open hands* at temples, then swing out away from temples to form the "antlers" of a moose.

Child may touch temples with fingertips or lift both *open hands* above her shoulders.

ZEBRA

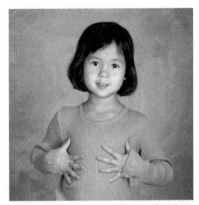

Both *open hands* are pulled across the body to show the zebra's "stripes."

Child may pat chest with *open hands.*

WHAT?

Gently shake open *cupped hands* with palms up and eyebrows raised.

Child may place hands with palms up or down in front of body and tilt head.

TIPS FOR INTRODUCING *THE ANIMAL FAIR*

○ Begin with the main characters of our story: the MONKEY and the ELEPHANT. Sign these two critters as they occur in the song. At the end of each verse, add the sign for WHAT? Make sure to use your best "question face" expression as you sign this word: raise your eyebrows, tilt your head, and do what comes naturally to you when you ask a question. You may need to peek in a mirror to determine your unique facial expression when asking questions in order to understand what your child sees as he watches you sing and sign the song.

○ Even toddlers love a good bouncing song. Place your child on your knees facing you with his legs straddling your thighs. As you hold his hands or back for stability, gently bounce him to the beat of this rollicking song. This circus tune musically simulates the sound of a carousel, so add adventure to your "horsey ride" by occasionally shifting your child on your legs from side to side. He will feel off balance and will hold on to your hands to right himself. Bouncing is great for *vestibular stimulation,* or the shifting of fluid in the inner ears, which influences a child's balance and coordination.

○ Placing your child in your lap facing you is also a great way to be close to your child as he imitates your motions for the animal signs. You can help him by using your own fingers to form the signs with his hands. Add a gentle bounce by lifting your heels up and down to the beat. This won't distract from signing but will enhance your "motor baby's" fun and engagement in the song.

♪ More Musical Fun with *The Animal Fair*

● "The Animal Fair" is a ballad and your child will enjoy hearing the story. Place your child in your lap with his back to your chest. Listen to the song without singing, and perform the animal signs in front of him. He may want to place his hands on yours and take a little "sign language ride," enjoying the motions without having to perform them himself.

● Play a silly pantomime game with "The Animal Fair." Sing or say the lyrics of the song without the CD so that you have the freedom to enjoy the song at your own pace and can stop as you like. Combine some of the animal signs with actions such as dancing, sneezing, combing your hair, falling on your knees, and tickling. Be certain to chuckle at your silly toddler's antics as he acts out the story!

● We made many farm animal sounds at "Grandpa's Farm." Now it is time to move like the animals at "The Animal Fair." Sway side to side while swinging your trunk like an ELEPHANT, bend your knees and swing your arms like a MONKEY, flap your wings and "fly" like a BIRD, and so on. Learning to perform these motions is actually "sign language" in the sense that we are using a gesture or set of gestures to represent an animal word. With the ASL signs we teach, the gestures are confined to the space in front of our torso. Engaging your toddler in this free-movement play can provide the link to the label—or animal's name—and then to a smaller and more precise gesture we call sign language.

Maia enjoys sign language by touching her mother's fingers as she performs the motions.

GAMES AND ACTIVITIES

♪ Beanie Critter in a Box

VOCABULARY PRACTICE: animal words, color words, **HIDE**

DEVELOPMENTAL BENEFITS: labeling animals and colors, planned motor motions, matching

MATERIALS: Beanie or other small stuffed animals; pictures of animals; boxes with lids; wrapping, butcher, or Con-Tact paper

Beanie Critter in a Box

DIRECTIONS: "Beanie" versions of animals can be found at garage sales or dollar stores and are great for teaching animal words. The toy versions are fun, tangible, and fairly realistic versions of actual animals. To prepare for this game, use plain boxes with tops, or cover the boxes with solid-color paper. Find pictures of animals in a magazine, or use your computer to print the animal pictures. Trim the photographs and paste them onto the lid of your box. Find an animal picture to match each of your beanie animals.

To begin the game, place two boxes in front of your child. Tell him it is time for the MONKEY to go to bed. He needs to find his own special box. Ask your toddler to put MONKEY in the monkey's box. See if he will match the monkey beanie animal to the box with the monkey picture by putting the animal inside. Repeat for other animals: can your toddler match the beanie animal to his box "bed?"

To make the task more difficult, give your child several beanie animals in a pile and ask him to "put the animals in their box beds." You can also wrap boxes in paper of different colors and ask him to put "HIPPO in the ORANGE bed" or "GIRAFFE in the GREEN box." Most toddlers I know think this is more fun than a box full of monkeys!

♪ Critters in Cups

VOCABULARY PRACTICE: animal words, **WHAT?**
DEVELOPMENTAL BENEFITS: sorting, fine-motor skills, tactile sensory experience
MATERIALS: muffin baking pan, animal crackers, fruit yogurt or applesauce

DIRECTIONS: We like food we can "do" at our house. We love to dip, dunk, and play with our food, and we especially like to lick our fingers. Critters in Cups is as much for enjoyment as it is for educational benefit. Place a muffin pan in front of your child. Give him a small pile of animal crackers and show him how to sort the animals into the cups of the pan: MONKEYS all go together in one cup, ELEPHANTS in another, and so on. Show him how to tell the difference between the cookies by looking at their shape and design.

Some toddlers will adore this animal cracker sorting activity. Others will enjoy putting crackers in the muffin pan cups without sorting. If your toddler is one of those who would prefer to *eat* his snack rather than *study* it, skip directly to the eating step. Fill one of the muffin pan cups

The animal crackers fit perfectly in this "child-sized" mini-muffin pan.

with yogurt or applesauce, and let him dip the animal crackers before gobbling them up. This messy critter consumption also has its benefits: it is great sensory stimulation for toddler fingertips. As your child eats each animal cracker, sing an ode to the one just consumed: "WHAT became of the GIRAFFE, the GIRAFFE? WHAT became of the GIRAFFE?"

♪ More Beanie Animal Fun: A Circus Train!

VOCABULARY PRACTICE: animal words, **PLAY, TRAIN***

DEVELOPMENTAL BENEFITS: imaginative play, motor planning

MATERIALS: scissors or paper punch; four or five recyclables for "train cars," such as milk jugs, two-liter pop bottles, and drum-shaped oatmeal boxes, plastic jars and bowls; beanie animals; yarn; washcloths or dishtowels and cardboard box (optional)

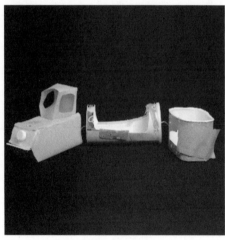

Circus Train

DIRECTIONS: Beanie animals love to ride in a circus train, and creating a train for your toddler to enjoy is easy. Using a paper punch or scissors, make a hole on either side of your recyclable containers. Attach the "train cars" by tying one to the next with yarn. Make sure each "car" is large enough and open on top to allow a beanie animal to fit inside. Some modifications may be necessary by cutting the container to make the "car" shorter. You might want to set up a "track" for the train with washcloths or dishtowels. A large cardboard box makes a great tunnel or train station. Ask your child if he would like to PLAY with your ANIMAL TRAIN.

Watch and see: your child will love this toy train as much as the versions commercially available for toddlers that cost hundreds of dollars!

---

* This bonus sign is found in the *Toddler Sing & Sign* Dictionary (page 207).

A SIGN OF SUCCESS

♪ *TODDLER SING & SIGN* HELPS TODDLERS DEVELOP ♪

We are all born with wonderful gifts. We use these gifts to express ourselves, to amuse, to strengthen, and to communicate. We begin as children
to explore and develop our talents, often unaware that we are unique, that
not everyone can do what we're doing!

—LYNN JOHNSTON

Music has a place in the life of a child. It helps with all kinds of learning; children can master social, language, and motor skills; basic concepts; participation skills; and more through the use of music. Every youngster should have the opportunity to learn music, and the years before children enter kindergarten are critical for their musical development. This is particularly true for those who are not developing typically. Whether music is used as a reward, a means of response, or simply a source of enjoyment, music enhances the world of a child with special needs.

The term "developmental delay" is used to refer to children who are behind schedule in meeting the milestones of childhood in areas including communication (understanding and using words), motor movement (rolling over, crawling, walking), and social inter-action (making eye contact, acknowledging others, accepting and returning affection). When a child exhibits developmental delays or medical or behavioral conditions that require educational services in order for him to benefit from his school experience, he is said to have "special needs."

There are circumstances when parents know before their child is born—or shortly after the baby arrives—that the child might have a medical condition or syndrome that will likely affect his or her learning potential. When Dana received the results of a blood test during her first trimester of pregnancy, she knew there was a slight chance that her son, Keaton, might have Down syndrome. When he was born, in Dana's words, "My husband went over and started taking pictures of Keaton, then he brought the camera back to me so I could see him. I had a C-section, so all I could do was look at the picture. I knew right then and there that he was born with Down syndrome. My heart dropped to the ground and I could not speak. That night after he was born all I did was cry. I was scared and did not know what to do with a child born with 'special needs.' I had a 'pity party' for myself, and then something just kicked into gear and I quit crying. I wanted to learn everything I could about Down syndrome. More importantly, I wanted to hold my precious, beautiful baby boy—and I did."

For many parents, the realization that their child may have learning challenges is a gradual process. Even the pediatrician may initially dismiss a parent's suspicions that the child is not developing as he should. This was the case with Deb, who intuitively recognized that her son Drew had a learning disability. She was particularly frustrated by doctors and therapists who dismissed her concerns as being "overly motherly" or advised her that "boys will be boys" and are therefore less likely to be able to focus on fine-motor tasks and skills requiring concentration and memorization. After seeking a professional evaluation Deb was able to not only receive a diagnosis for her son but to also discover exactly what his strengths and challenges were.

However, this information wasn't helpful in determining what to do to help Drew. She used Drew's interest and ability in large-motor movement to engage him in learning his letters. Together they drew letters in shaving cream, in the sandbox, and even with flashlights on the wall of their darkened garage. Through these types of motor and sensory activities, Drew showed his mother that although he was unable to demonstrate his knowledge of the letters of the alphabet in conventional ways, such as pointing to them in a book or drawing them with crayons on paper, he truly knew them.

If parents suspect that their child is not meeting developmental milestones, or if they observe medical or behavioral symptoms that concern them, it is important to get a professional evaluation. This process can be initiated by working with a pediatrician or local Parents as Teachers (PAT) program, who can assist in a referral to the local Infant and Toddler Services (ITS). These are free programs that are available in every community. In the case of a child who is three years of age or older, local school districts are the best first contact.

The ITS program or school district may first perform a screening to determine if evaluation is appropriate. Your knowledge of what your child can and can not do, as well as concerns you may have, will be important pieces of the screening and, if needed, evaluation. The results of the evaluation will help determine if your child is progressing within a typical range of development or if there is a developmental delay or disability that will require support from professionals, such as an occupational therapist and speech-language pathologist. If this support is necessary, parents and professionals work together as a team to develop a plan, which includes goals or outcomes and a description of the services necessary to work toward those goals or outcomes. The plan is reviewed on a regular basis and adjusted according to the needs of the child and the family. Early intervention is critical to help a child achieve his learning potential.

Can *Toddler Sing & Sign* help toddlers with developmental delays? DeLynn C. Jenkins is a licensed social worker and works as an early educational specialist for a large suburban school district. She helps toddlers transition at three years of age into preschool programs that serve special-needs children. As a parent of three who has worked extensively with toddlers who have learning struggles, she advises, "Exposing toddlers with developmental delays to a program that incorporates music, sign language, play-based activity and rich picture book literature is not only beneficial but a best practice. Research has shown that programs that incorporate these crucial components help to promote self-esteem, self-discipline and creativity in all children. More specifically, it allows children that are not able to communicate verbally an opportunity to communicate through music, movement, sign and pictures."

Further, *Toddler Sing & Sign* enhances the parent-child interactions necessary for early intervention to be effective, notes Kendall Burr, an early childhood interventionist for infants and toddlers with disabilities. "I think there is a belief that these interactions are supposed to come naturally, but in many families this is just not the case. Programs like *Toddler Sing & Sign* provide support for parents and caregivers, and can give them the confidence to follow their instincts." This, in Kendall's experience, leads parents and caregivers to take a more active role in their child's intervention program.

The benefits of the *Toddler Sing & Sign* program are extensive for the preschool child with special needs, as well. According to Dr. Cynthia M. Colwell, director of music therapy at the University of Kansas, "*Toddler Sing & Sign* incorporates a focus on language learning with attention to other developmental goals such as concentrated listening and sustained attention, large- and fine-motor coordination, cognitive enhancement, and social interaction. All of these nonmusical areas are addressed through a parent-child engagement model that supports the budding young musician."

> Music and sign language provide powerful and important ways to communicate and connect with others, regardless of ability or disability.

Through folk repertoire, rearranged and freshened to incorporate signing and motor response, children with special needs are immersed in an educational program—but are actually just responding to music they love. According to the folk musician and music critic Lahri Bond, the *Toddler Sing & Sign* music CD contains "very musical and intelligent arrangements—playing 'for' children instead of 'at' them." The tunes are timeless and meant to be enjoyed by children—and adults—of all ages.

Jennifer Ferguson, a special-needs preschool teacher, agrees. She believes that these music and sign language activities enrich the learning experiences for all of her students, especially

Keaton and his mother, Dana, share their special "love language" of sign and song.

those with autism, speech disorders, and overall developmental delays. She observed enhanced learning for her typically developing peer models, and even more significant progress for students with special needs. An exciting increase in language and communication skills was observed as a result of using music and sign language in her classroom. Students with social and behavioral concerns also blossomed when she utilized music.

Says Jennifer, "*Toddler Sing & Sign* is motivating and fun. I am certain that music is the glue for learning. It engages young children emotionally and pulls them into the activity. The combination of music and sign involves many of their senses in the learning process, which assists in retention. It makes the new information 'stick.' The usage of music and sign language is effective for social interactions, too. It creates a common focus while enhancing participation and increasing communication skills. *Toddler Sing & Sign* supports my efforts in making learning fun for all of my students."

The goal of this book is to create activities that you can enjoy with your child while connecting with him in a more meaningful way. While research does suggest that the use of signing can enhance the overall communication skills for children, this may not be the case for every child. The activities and information in this book are in no way intended to substitute for the expertise and assistance of a speech-language pathologist and are not meant to replace speech or language therapy. If you have any concerns about the development of your child, particularly in the area of communication, please talk to your pediatrician or contact your local school district for screening information.

Music and sign language provide powerful and important ways to communicate and connect with others, regardless of ability or disability. Mr. Fred Rogers spoke fondly of music when he said, "Finding ways to harmonize our uniqueness with the uniqueness of others can be the most fun—and most rewarding of all." I teach music and sign language, and some of my students have been identified as having special needs. However, I have never met a young child who doesn't have "special needs." Each is unique in her strengths and challenges, her favorite foods and colors, the way she prefers to learn, what makes her laugh out loud, and the unique way she looks at her world.

No two people—or voices or songs—are identical. Celebrate the unique and amazing qualities of your child.

BOOKS TO READ

I dare you to try to keep from tapping your toe to Debbie Harter's "jungle beat" as you read her lively picture book *The Animal Boogie* (Barefoot Books). You'll wish you had a conga drum to play along as you rhythmically read. Practice reading this story a time or two before you share it with your toddler so that you read with the proper syncopation and enthusiasm. This book is probably not a candidate for soothing your little beastie off to bed, as these animals like to "boogie, woogie, and oogie!" Shake your tail feathers with *The Animal Boogie* while the sun is still shining.

ANIMAL

Animals (All Change!) by Angela Lambert (Child's Play International)

Bright Baby Animals by Roger Priddy (Priddy Books)

Animal Kisses by Barney Saltzberg (Red Wagon Books)

I Love Animals Big Book by Flora McDonnell (Candlewick Press)

My First Animal Book by Anne Millard (DK Preschool)

BIRD

Counting Is for the Birds by Frank Mazzola Jr. (Charlesbridge)

Hello, Little Bird by Petr Horacek (Walker Books)

I Heard, Said the Bird by Polly Berrien Berends (Puffin Books)

The Lion and the Little Red Bird by Elisa Kleven (Puffin Books)

The Baby Beebee Bird by Diane Redfield Massie (HarperCollins)

BABOON/MONKEY

Baboon by Kate Banks (Farrar, Straus and Giroux)

Eight Silly Monkeys by Steve Haskamp (Intervisual Books)

Naughty Little Monkeys by Jim Aylesworth (Dutton Juvenile)

Soon, Baboon, Soon by Dave Horowitz (Putnam Juvenile)

Zoo Parade! by Harriet Ziefert (Blue Apple)

ELEPHANT

Elephant (Proud Parents) by Pam Adams (Child's International)

Polite Elephant by Richard Scarry (Golden Books)

"Stand Back," Said the Elephant, "I'm Going to Sneeze!" by Patricia Thomas (HarperCollins)

The Saggy Baggy Elephant by Kathryn Jackson and Byron Jackson (Golden Books)

The Ant and the Elephant by Bill Peet (Houghton Mifflin)

HIPPO

But Not the Hippopotamus by Sandra Boynton (Little Simon)

Hattie Hippo by Christine Loomis (Orchard Books)

Hippo-not-amus by Tony Payne and Jan Payne (Orchard Books)

Hippos Go Berserk! by Sandra Boynton (Little Simon)

The Hiccuping Hippo by Keith Faulkner (Dial Books)

GIRAFFE

I'm a Little Giraffe by Tim Weare (Cartwheel Books)

Jessica Giraffe's Long Neck by Christine Harder (Standard Publishing)

New Baby Giraffe by Laura Gates Galvin and Jesse Cohen (Soundprints)

The Giraffe Who Cock-A-Doodle-Doo'd by Keith Faulkner (Dial Books)

The Green Giraffe by Margaret S. Campilonga (Chicken Soup Press)

MOOSE

Busy, Busy Moose by Nancy Van Laan (Houghton Mifflin)

Elusive Moose by Joan Gannij (Barefoot Books)

If You Give a Moose a Muffin by Laura Numeroff (Laura Geringer/HarperCollins)

Moose on the Loose by John Hassett (Down East Books)

One Moose, Twenty Mice by Clare Beaton (Barefoot Books)

ZEBRA

How the Zebra Got Its Stripes by Golden Books (Golden Books)

On Beyond Zebra! by Dr. Seuss (Random House Books for Young Readers)

Zebra Clops! by Stephen Barker (Campbell Books)

Zebra's Rainbow by Bang on the Door! (Oxford University Press)

Zoe and Her Zebra by Clare Beaton (Barefoot Books)

WHAT?

Jesse Bear, What Will You Wear? by Nancy White Carlstrom (Aladdin)

What Bounces? by Kate Duke (Dutton Juvenile)

What Can You Do In the Rain? by Anna Grossnickle Hines (Greenwillow Books)

What Do You Say? by Mandy Stanley (Little Simon)

What's the Opposite, PiggyWiggy? by Christyan and Diane Fox (Hand Print)

8

THE LION SLEEPS TONIGHT ("WIMOWEH")

ANIMAL WORD TO LEARN: **LION**
COLOR WORD TO LEARN: **YELLOW**
OTHER WORDS TO LEARN: **JUNGLE/TREES, QUIET/HUSH**
BONUS WORDS: **VILLAGE/TOWN***
WORDS TO REVIEW: **AFRAID*, MUSIC/SONG*, SLEEP***

This South African Zulu hunting song was written by Solomon Linda and evolved into an American classic when Alan Lomax, a musicologist, shared a recording of this tune with his friend Pete Seeger. Mr. Seeger told me that he believed Linda was singing "Wee-moo-weh" when he heard the original recording. Actually, Linda was singing "Mbube" or "Mmmm-boo-beh," which means the "lion is sleeping." However, Seeger's pronunciation of the title lyric has endured. Seeger and his folk band, The Weavers, recorded "Wimoweh" in 1952. Many other renditions were recorded, under the titles of "Mbube," "Wimoweh," and "The Lion Sleeps Tonight." The Tokens took a rendition with English lyrics to the top of the pop charts in 1961.

Chorus:
Wee dee dee dee . . . Wimoweh!   *Sign MUSIC*
Wee dee dee dee . . . Wimoweh!   *Sign MUSIC*
Wimoweh. . . .   *Sign MUSIC or dance!*

Verse 1:
In the JUNGLE, the mighty JUNGLE,   *Sign JUNGLE*
The LION SLEEPS tonight.   *Sign LION or LION SLEEPS*
In the JUNGLE, the QUIET JUNGLE,
The LION SLEEPS tonight.   *Sign LION or LION SLEEPS*

---

* These bonus signs are found in the *Toddler Sing & Sign* Dictionary (page 207).

Chorus: Wee dee . . . Wimoweh . . .	*Sign MUSIC or dance!*
Verse 2:	
Near the VILLAGE,	*Sign VILLAGE*
The peaceful [QUIET] VILLAGE,	*Sign QUIET*
The LION SLEEPS tonight,	*Sign LION or LION SLEEPS*
Near the VILLAGE,	*Sign VILLAGE*
The peaceful VILLAGE,	*Sign QUIET*
The LION SLEEPS tonight!	*Sign LION or LION SLEEPS*
Chorus: Wee dee . . . Wimoweh . . .	*Sign MUSIC or dance!*
Verse 3:	
Hush [QUIET] my darling,	*Sign QUIET*
Don't fear [AFRAID], my darling,	*Sign AFRAID*
The LION SLEEPS tonight,	*Sign LION or LION SLEEPS*
Hush [QUIET] my darling,	*Sign QUIET*
Don't fear [AFRAID], my darling,	*Sign AFRAID*
The LION SLEEPS tonight!	*Sign LION or LION SLEEPS*
Hey, hey!	
Whoa . . . Wimoweh!	*Sign MUSIC or dance!*
Chorus: Wee dee dee dee . . . Wimoweh . . .	*Sign MUSIC or dance!*

THE LION SLEEPS TONIGHT ("WIMOWEH")

Based on a song by Solomon Linda and Paul Campbell
Lyrics by George David Weiss, Hugo Peretti, and Luigi Creatore
© 1961, renewed Abilene Music, LLC
Permission secured. All rights reserved.

LION

Starting at forehead, one open *cupped hand* moves over top of head, showing the lion's "mane."

Child may touch or pat top of head with hand.

YELLOW

Extend thumb and little finger of *closed fist* and twist back and forth at wrist.

Child may shake *open hand* or *closed fist* with only thumb extended.

**JUNGLE/
TREES**

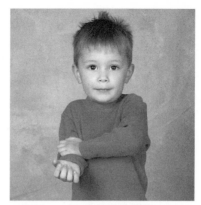

Place elbow of *open hand* on top of other hand. While rotating wrist of *open hand*, move arms in front of body from one side to the other.

Child may move one or both hands in chopping motion across body, or place one hand on top of the other without movement.

QUIET/HUSH

Hold one pointer finger at lips, then draw both *closed hands* down and out in a calming motion.

Child may hold pointer finger to lips without performing the second motion.

TIPS FOR INTRODUCING
THE LION SLEEPS TONIGHT

○ The key vocabulary words to teach your toddler are LION, SLEEP, and MUSIC. Start with LION and practice signing this word as it occurs in the song. MUSIC can be signed any time you aren't singing words of the story. The high falsetto voice you hear on the CD can be imitated by your toddler with practice.

○ When you sing about the "QUIET VILLAGE" or "HUSH, my darling," use a quiet singing voice. This is another instance where sign and song support toddler's understanding of intangible concepts such as loud and soft, high and low, fast and slow. The sign language gives the child a concrete way to represent these dimensions, and music provides the direct experience.

○ It is great fun to dance to all the choruses of this wonderful song. There was a good reason The Tokens took this song to the top of the dance charts in 1961. Get in touch with your fancy-dancing toddler self and strut your stuff as you sing "Wimoweh." You are welcome to sign the verses to each other much like a "hand jive" you would mirror with a dance partner.

♪ ## More Musical Fun with *The Lion Sleeps Tonight*

Lettie and her father dance to
"Wimoweh" in their backyard "jungle."

● One of the goals of signing with toddlers is for them to begin to combine words and signs into short phrases. LION SLEEPS is a great phrase for toddlers to sign, and there are plenty of repetitions within the song for mastery of this two-word combination.

● For very young children, singing is more a sensation than a sound. When your child sings the "weeee!" part of the "Wimoweh" chorus, praise her for her beautiful singing. The sound may not be what you expect, but your child is expressing her musical self as she learns to imitate in her own way all of the sounds she is hearing.

● With each repetition of the "Wimoweh" chorus at the end of the song, try to dance lower and sing more quietly. Finish the song by sitting on the floor and hugging your lion cub.

GAMES AND ACTIVITIES

♪ Jungle Jingler Wand

VOCABULARY PRACTICE: color words, **MUSIC, QUIET/HUSH, HIDE, JUNGLE**

DEVELOPMENTAL BENEFITS: listening skills, combining words, motor planning, awareness of fast and slow

MATERIALS: 6-inch wooden dowel, smoothly sanded, ½-inch metal eyelet with screw, 8 feet of ¼-inch-wide satin or grosgrain ribbon in one or more colors, one large jingle bell, one nail, and a hammer for starting a hole for the metal eyelet screw

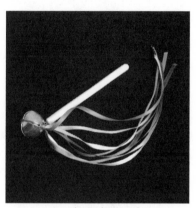

Jungle Jingler Wand

DIRECTIONS: Feed the jingle bell onto the metal eyelet. You may need to bend the eyelet slightly with pliers to fit the bell onto the eyelet, and then bend the eyelet again to its original position once the bell is securely in the eyelet. Using a hammer, tap the nail into the end of the dowel. Pull the nail out and insert the end of the eyelet screw into this hole. Screw the eyelet tightly into the top of the dowel. Cut the ribbon into four pieces, each measuring two feet long. Lay all four on top of each other with ends matching. Then gather them in your hand and thread them through the eyelet. Tie them in a knot. You now have a colorful Jungle Jingler.

You can choose to make yours with only yellow-colored ribbon and call it your Yellow Jungle Jingler, signing YELLOW MUSIC for your toddler. You can also make a rainbow version with several colors of ribbon. You might want to make a set of Jungle Jinglers so that every family member can play along—and create them each with their own special color. This would be great for practicing listening skills and identifying colors ("find the GREEN MUSIC Jingler!").

Sing "The Lion Sleeps Tonight" and show your toddler how to play your Jungle Jingler throughout the song. You can also play only when you hear the "Wee . . . Wimoweh" choruses of the song. Play softly when you sing about the "QUIET VILLAGE" or "HUSH, my darling!"

Another fun game is a version of hide-and-seek where you hide with your

Gianni makes beautiful music with his Jungle Jingler Wand.

Jungle Jingler and the child finds you by listening for the jingle-bell sound. You could also add your singing voice ("Wimoweh!") to the jingle sound to help her find you. You can then change places with your child and listen for her Jungle Jingler as she waits for you to find her.

I recommend that you supervise your child carefully as you play with the Jungle Jingler. Please be certain your child does not run with this stick in hand. It is best to play the listening game indoors and to model a quiet and slow approach to your playing so that your toddler doesn't get overly stimulated and run or fall. Also, check the Jungle Jingler often to make sure the jingle bell doesn't become a choking hazard for your child. My version is made with a bell too large to fit through a toilet paper tube. This is a good way to decide if a toy is likely to pose a choking threat to your child. Toddlers are often past the mouthing stage by age two, but it is best to use caution.

♪ King of the Jungle Mask

VOCABULARY PRACTICE: **LION, SLEEP, YELLOW, ORANGE, BLACK**
DEVELOPMENTAL BENEFITS: imaginary play, fine-motor development
MATERIALS: paper plate, orange and yellow construction paper, scissors, glue. black marker

Children learn to play "pretend" by wearing props and masks such as the Lion Paper Plate Mask.

DIRECTIONS: you can't be the King of the Jungle if you don't look the part. Follow these simple steps to create a lion mask fit for a king.

Cut out a yellow circle to fit the center of your paper plate. This will be the face. Using the black marker, draw large expressive eyes, a bold triangular nose (an upside-down triangle), and a round *W*-shaped mouth on the yellow circle face. Add whiskers to your face as well. Use your scissors to cut a small hole in each eye so that your child can see out when wearing the mask.

Now cut your orange construction paper into strips of varying length (some approximately 1 x 4 inches and some 1 x 7 inches). Help your child wrap the orange strips tightly around your marker to "curl" your paper for the lion's mane. Put glue on one end of the orange curls, and place them all around the outer edge of your paper plate face. You may add short pieces of orange and yellow yarn and ribbon to your mane and use the scraps of your yellow paper to make ears to glue at the top of your lion's face, too.

Once the glue on your lion mask is dry, you are ready to be the King of the Jungle. Grab your mask, turn on the song "The Lion Sleeps Tonight," and practice your best lion strut as you parade around your home. Pretend to sleep when you hear "the LION SLEEPS tonight." Take turns pretending to be the lion king with your lion cub, or make two masks so that you can both be lions at the same time. Your lion cub will roar with glee to have this pretend play opportunity with you!

♪ Don't Wake the Lion!

VOCABULARY PRACTICE: **HUSH/QUIET, SLEEP, LION**
DEVELOPMENTAL BENEFITS: imaginary play, parent-child bond, large-motor movements
MATERIALS: floor space; blanket; anything "lionlike," such as a stuffed animal, a miniature character, a paper plate mask, or even a homemade costume using a headband with lion ears, a furry or fuzzy scarf as the mane, mittens, and a tube-sock tail

DIRECTIONS: Put on your imagination cap, because it's time for *you* to become a lion. Place the blanket in the middle of the floor space designated for the game. Have your child stand at the edge of the blanket. While holding or wearing your lion prop, crouch in the middle of the blanket. Act catlike and give a tame roar. Lie down and pretend to sleep. Tell your lion cub that the lion is going to sleep, so she will need to be quiet as she walks around the blanket. Now chant the words "the LION SLEEPS, the LION SLEEPS, the LION SLEEPS tonight." When you say "tonight," catch your lion cub and give her a hug and a tickle

Isaac and his mom have fun playing the Don't Wake the Lion game.

You and your child can take turns being the lion so that she can try to catch you. In addition, you can repeat the chant more than once in a turn and watch your child as she anticipates on which "tonight" you will wake. Play again and again until your child begins to tire. For the grand finale, turn on the song "The Lion Sleeps Tonight," and dance and sing loudly with your lion cub. Use exaggerated movements and act silly. Roar to your hearts' content!

A SIGN OF SUCCESS

♪ GETTING READY FOR PRESCHOOL ♪
WITH *TODDLER SING & SIGN*

Parents and caregivers want to prepare toddlers for success in preschool. We know that the years between birth and age five are critical for all kinds of learning. Even before a child attends school, she is learning skills that will help her with reading, writing, and mathematics. These skills include:

- ○ **Phonological awareness.** The child hears the sounds in spoken words and understands the relationship of these sounds (sounds made for each letter in a word, syllables within words, words in sentences, etc.).
- ○ **Print awareness.** The child notices that the print on the page actually represents spoken words. She may begin to touch the written words as she hears them being read to her in a book.
- ○ **Rhyming.** The child hears that single-syllable words start with different letter sounds, but sound the same at the end, such as beach and teach.
- ○ **Visual discrimination.** The child's ability to determine visually subtle distinguishing characteristics among various objects. For instance, the young child can look at two pictures on a page and tell that they are different or alike, or see someone sign two different words and notice they are not the same. She may also be able to label them ("dog," "turtle"). Eventually she will see differences in written letters and words.
- ○ **Vocabulary.** The number of words a child knows or uses to express herself, including signed and spoken words, is steadily growing.
- ○ **Sequencing.** The child observes that objects are arranged in a certain order and can often anticipate what comes next in the series.
- ○ **Patterning.** Once a child observes the arranged sequence of objects, she can add more objects in accordance with the design or plan.

And all of these are developmental benefits your child will experience through the *Toddler Sing & Sign* program.

For a kindergartner, practicing *phonological awareness* means knowing that the word "cat" is made of three sounds: /k/, /a/, /t/. For a toddler, this means hearing phrases like "sitting on the bank with my dog named Blue, honey," and knowing that even though it is sung quickly, the phrase is made up of individual words. Toddlers also practice phonological awareness when singing about a *fox* and a *box*. Rhyming teaches that changing only one sound can make a completely different word—an important concept for decoding words later on.

Print awareness develops when a parent reads from the book while singing and signing along to "The Crawdad Song." It also happens when, after singing "The Crawdad Song," Dad reads *In the Small, Small Pond* from the recommended book list. Pointing out that the word "fish" in the book is connected to saying, singing, and signing FISH is yet another example.

Rhyming words appeal to the toddler's sense of humor and whimsy as you sing about the "BEAR in the CHAIR" in "All Around the Kitchen," as well as "The Animal Fair" song, where "the ELEPHANT SNEEZED and fell on his KNEES!" Your toddler may begin to fill in the blank if you read her the first phrase containing a rhyming word and let her say or sign you the second rhyming word where it occurs in the phrase.

The visual nature of sign language is wonderful for practicing *visual discrimination* skills. Before the child can begin to use signs expressively, she must first be able to see that the signs you show her as you speak are in fact each different. This is a necessary prerequisite skill before she can assign meaning to the gestures and use them to communicate with you. The visual discrimination skills necessary to tell the sign for BEAR from the sign for LION will later help your child know that *R* is different from *H*.

Parents who speak often about a variety of topics of interest to their children tend to have toddlers with a rich *vocabulary*. The use of books and music exposes children to words not used in everyday conversation. The rich variety of words and sounds used in music, particularly the music in *Toddler Sing & Sign,* can help to build the broad vocabulary necessary for developing strong skills not only in reading but also in writing, speaking, and listening. The child development experts Betty Hart and Todd Risely found that parent-child interactions are the most important factor in the development of vocabulary. Two critical components that were identified as a result of the study are the *number of total words* spoken to children each day, and the *number of different words* spoken to children.

> The rich variety of words and ideas used in music, particularly the music in *Toddler Sing & Sign,* can help to build the broad vocabulary necessary for strong skills not only in reading but also in writing, speaking, and listening.

While *sequencing* and *patterning* are important skills for reading, they are also critical for the development of mathematical thinking. When a child learns to predict that the chorus is coming in the song "Down on Grandpa's Farm," she is using the same part of the brain that will enable her later to organize information to solve mathematical equations.

Reading and talking to your child are essential experiences. Children learn best while relating with caring adults. It is the number and quality of those social contacts that helps toddlers learn and grow in every way, including mastering skills for later school success.

Here are some tips for supporting your child's language and literacy:

○ **Talk to your toddler. And then talk some more. Talk about what you see, what you are doing, what you are thinking about . . .**
- ◆ Signing with your child gives your words more meaning, because you are combining what he sees with what he hears. Pictures or objects accomplish this as well.
- ◆ Let your inner Food Network TV star come out. Talk about the steps you are taking while you make oatmeal, grilled cheese, or pizza.
- ◆ Talk about what you are doing and why. "I'm writing down all of the things we need from the grocery store on this list so that we won't forget."
- ◆ Comment on what you see your child do. "Look at what you built! You used lots of big blocks on the bottom and small blocks on the top."

○ **Listen to your toddler.**
- ◆ When she comments on her world, affirm and expand, like this . . .
    Child: "Tuk!"
    Parent: "Yes, Lizzie, I see the truck. It's a big, blue dump truck. That truck is full of dirt!"
- ◆ When she asks questions, give an answer that leads to more questions or comments. Help your child practice the turn taking involved in conversation.

○ **Use everyday tasks.**
- ◆ It might not feel as efficient, but letting your child help with everyday tasks gives her a sense of responsibility, and might even make your job go faster, because you won't have to stop to redirect a bored toddler!
- ◆ You have to fold the laundry anyway, so ask your toddler to help by finding all of the socks in the basket. Then let her help you by matching the like socks. Ask her to find Daddy's blue shirt, Mommy's brown pants, etc., in the basket of clean clothes.

- ◆ Unloading forks and spoons from the dishwasher and helping put them away and taking plastic and paper recyclables to the bin are great sorting activities.

⚪ **Create a routine.**

- ◆ Knowing what to expect in her day helps your toddler feel secure and sets the stage for learning throughout the day.
- ◆ Music is a natural for cueing routines. Always singing or playing "All Around the Kitchen" while you make dinner lets your child know mealtime is coming next.
- ◆ For frequent or favorite trips, notice landmarks along the way. On the way to grandpa's farm, we see the pond first, then the train station, then we cross the bridge over the river, then we turn on the gravelly road. On the way to school, we see the tennis courts, then the fountains . . .
- ◆ Mark time with music. Time concepts are difficult for children, but they can begin to anticipate how long it will take to get to Gianni's house if you tell them, "It will take twenty minutes. That's about how long it takes to listen to all of the songs until 'The Animal Fair.'" Or make it a game. " I think we can be done putting away toys before 'Grizzly Bear' is over. What do you think?"

⚪ **Make connections.**

- ◆ Young children are constantly seeking order in the new things they learn.
- ◆ Helping your child discover what is the same and different about two favorite parks, different neighborhood dogs, socks, trees, etc., can help expand her understanding of her world.
- ◆ Use the same signs in different settings so that your child can figure out that a word isn't specific to a specific location. Sign TRUCK for the toy variety at your house, the one pictured in her truck book, as well as variety of trucks your toddler sees out of the car window as you drive.

⚪ **Follow your child's lead.**

- ◆ One day, your child is driving you nuts because she wants to play the rhyming game ad nauseam. The next day, she has no interest in it. She is a typical toddler.
- ◆ Just when you think she is bored with a toy or game and has outgrown it, it suddenly becomes her favorite again. She is a typical toddler.

Children master speech, problem solving, skills for independence, and their expression of love and compassion for others through interactions with the caring people in their world. Keep your "home schooling" playful and fun, and your child will *choose* to learn.

—Kendall Burr, child development specialist and mother of two

Dad is fostering literacy as well as language development by spending time reading to Eleanor and Avery.

BOOKS TO READ

"In the jungle, the quiet jungle, the baby lion cub sleeps tonight. . . ." Or at least he tries to sleep while other jungle animals threaten to wake him in this picture book by Paul Bright titled *The Loudest Lion* (Scholastic). You will have twenty-five opportunities to practice your QUIET sign as you read this story about lion parents who try to help their baby sleep undisturbed. The surprise ending will make you laugh very loudly!

LION

If I Were a Lion by Sarah Weeks (Atheneum)

Leo the Late Bloomer by Robert Kraus (Harper-Trophy)

Randy's Dandy Lions by Bill Peet (Houghton Mifflin)

That's Not My Lion by Fiona Watt (Educational Development Corporation)

We're Going on a Lion Hunt by David Axtell (Henry Holt)

YELLOW

Blue, Blue and Yellow, Too by Biruta Hansen (National Geographic Children's Books)

Fuzzy Yellow Ducklings by Matthew Van Fleet (Ragged Bears)

One Yellow Lion by Matthew Van Fleet (Dial Books)

Red Lace, Yellow Lace by Mark Casey and Judith Herbst (Barron's Educational Series)

Yellow Hippo by Alan Rogers (Two-Can)

JUNGLE/TREES

Jungle Jive by Sally Lloyd Jones (Silver Dolphin)

I Spy in the Jungle by Damon Burnard (Chronicle Books)

In the Jungle by Benedicte Guettier (Kane/Miller)

Peek-a-Boo Jungle by Francesca Ferri (Barron's Educational Series)

Walking Through the Jungle by Debbie Harter (Barefoot Books)

QUIET/HUSH

Hush, Little Ones by John Butler (Peachtree)

Please Be Quiet! by Mary Murphy (Houghton Mifflin)

Quiet Loud by Leslie Patricelli (Candlewick Press)

The Little Quiet Book by Katherine Ross (Random House Books for Young Readers)

The Very Quiet Cricket Board Book by Eric Carle (Philomel)

THE MOCKINGBIRD (HUSH LITTLE BABY)

ANIMAL WORDS TO LEARN: **GOAT, BULL/COW**
OTHER WORD TO LEARN: **SWEET**
WORDS TO REVIEW: **HORSE, QUIET/HUSH, BABY, MOMMY*, DADDY*, MUSIC/SING**
BONUS WORD: **LOUD***

This Southern Appalachian lullaby has lulled many sweet babies to sleep. Some versions have "Momma" singing; some have "Papa." We split the difference and include them both. Your toddler will hear both "Momma" and "Papa" singing her to sleep on the recording.

Verse 1:
HUSH [QUIET], LITTLE BABY, don't say a word,   *Sign QUIET*
MOMMA's gonna buy you a mockingBIRD.   *Sign MOMMY or*
                                                    MOMMY and BIRD

If that mockingBIRD don't sing,   *Sign BIRD or*
                                                    BIRD and SING

MOMMA's gonna buy you a diamond ring.   *Sign MOMMY*

Verse 2:
If that diamond ring turns to brass,
PAPA's gonna buy you a lookin' glass.   *Sign DADDY*
If that lookin' glass gets broke,
PAPA's gonna buy you a Billy GOAT.   *Sign GOAT or*
                                                    PAPA and GOAT

---

*   These bonus signs are found in the *Toddler Sing & Sign* Dictionary (page 207).

Verse 3:
If that Billy GOAT won't pull,   *Sign GOAT*
MOMMA's gonna buy you a cart and BULL.   *Sign BULL or*
                                                                 MOMMY and BULL

If that cart and BULL turn over,
PAPA's gonna buy you a DOG named Rover.   *Sign DOG or*
                                                                 DADDY and DOG

Chorus:
HUSH, LITTLE BABY,   *Sign BABY*
HUSH now,   *Sign QUIET*
HUSH, LITTLE BABY   *Sign BABY*
HUSH!   *Sign QUIET*
HUSH, LITTLE BABY   *Sign BABY*
HUSH now,   *Sign QUIET*
HUSH, LITTLE BABY   *Sign BABY*
HUSH!   *Sign QUIET*

Verse 4:
If that DOG named Rover won't bark,   *Sign DOG*
PAPA's gonna buy you a HORSE and cart.   *Sign HORSE or*
                                                                 DADDY and HORSE

If that HORSE and cart fall down,   *Sign HORSE*
You'll still be the SWEETEST LITTLE   *Sign SWEET*
BABY in TOWN.   *Sign BABY*

Repeat Chorus: HUSH, LITTLE BABY . . .

HUSH, LITTLE BABY, don't say a word,   *Sign QUIET*
MOMMA's gonna buy you a mockingBIRD.   *Sign BIRD or*
                                                                 MOMMY and BIRD

THE MOCKINGBIRD
(HUSH LITTLE BABY)

Traditional / Adapted by Anne Meeker Miller and Jeff Martin

GOAT

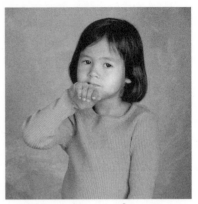

The backside of *two* bent *open fingers* taps chin, then forehead showing the goat's beard and horns.

Child may place or tap fingertips on forehead and then chin, or touch only forehead or chin.

BULL/COW

Place thumb at temple and rotate extended little finger down.

Child may touch temple with fingertips or *closed hand*. His sign for BULL/COW may look like his sign for DONKEY or HORSE.

SWEET

Brush fingertips of *closed hand* down chin from lips as if wiping away a sweet treat.

Child may place or tap fingertips on chin. His sign for SWEET may look like his sign for WATER or MOMMY.

TIPS FOR INTRODUCING *THE MOCKINGBIRD*

○ "The Mockingbird" is a snuggle song. The duet of male and female voices is meant to emulate the soothing singing of Mommy and Daddy. Hold your toddler with his back to your chest, and rock gently. You can listen together and tenderly sign MOMMY and DADDY in front of him as the male and female voices take turns singing on the recording.

○ Another variation is to sign only the repeating choruses ("HUSH, LITTLE BABY, HUSH now . . ."). The repetition and simple hand shapes required for those two signs make signing the music enjoyable and very musically expressive.

○ Animals are very motivating for toddlers to sign. To continue our animal theme, your toddler might enjoy signing all the animals you hear in the song.

♪ More Musical Fun with *The Mockingbird*

● The lullabies are found at the end of the *Toddler Sing & Sign* CD. You are encouraged to make music listening a part of your bedtime rituals, and to allow your child to fall asleep listening to our lullabies. Keep a small CD player in your child's bedroom. This will help to establish a routine and make your child feel he is not alone as he falls asleep.

● Hum along with the performance of the song on the CD. The resonance of your breastbone against your toddler's back is soothing to him. He will be unconsciously aware of your breathing as you hum the tune, and will enjoy the sensation as well as the sound of your song.

● Tell your toddler he is the "sweetest little baby in town" as you tuck him into bed!

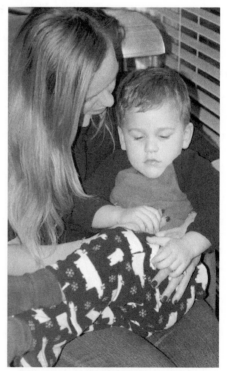

Bedtime is a perfect opportunity to sing, sign, and snuggle.

GAMES AND ACTIVITIES

♪ Don't Wake the Baby!

VOCABULARY PRACTICE: WALK, QUIET, SWEET, BABY, ANIMAL, SLEEP, LOUD*
DEVELOPMENTAL BENEFITS: awareness of loud and soft, imaginary play, purposeful motor movement, tactile sensory experience
MATERIALS: five 12-inch squares of bubble wrap (larger bubbles work best), scented lotion, small cushions

Austin and Rachel love the sensory experience of their foot massage.

DIRECTIONS: Make a path by alternating flat cushions and bubble wrap squares on the floor. Tell your child that you are going to take a walk in the woods. Tell him he is to walk quietly so that he won't wake up the baby animals who are sleeping. Hold your child's hand and help him step on the path of cushions and bubble wrap squares, alternating his feet (left, right, left, right) as he walks. Ask him to step quietly so that his feet don't make a sound. If he steps on the bubble wrap and pops a bubble, say, "So LOUD!" If he steps on the bubble wrap without popping bubbles, say, "So QUIET!" See if your child can control the pressure of his steps so that the bubbles won't break and wake up the baby animals. When it is time to WAKE the BABY ANIMALS, allow your child to give the bubble wrap a good stomping!

When he has finished his walk, rub his feet with the scented lotion. Tell him he has SWEET feet. Rub the lotion in between his toes and all over his feet. Pause to pretend to "eat" his "sweet feet." Hopefully he will be willing to reciprocate by giving your "sweet feet" a good massage! The sensory stimulation of the quiet walk in combination with the foot massage is wonderful for little feet learning to walk, run, jump, and dance.

---

* This bonus sign is found in the *Toddler Sing & Sign* Dictionary (page 201).

♪ Noisy Color Crunch

VOCABULARY PRACTICE: color words, **HIDE, HELP***

DEVELOPMENTAL BENEFITS: tactile sensory experience, fine motor skills, problem solving, concepts of in and out, errorless learning

MATERIALS: one roll each of a variety of colors of cellophane wrapping material, including red and blue; boxes and/or cloth bags

(Note: Do not use plastic bags when playing games with children.)

DIRECTIONS: To prepare for the game, cut a 36-inch square of red cellophane wrapping material. Stuff it into a small box or cloth bag. Repeat for the blue cellophane. You are now ready to play!

Noisy Color Crunch

Tell your child you have lost RED and don't know where it can be. It must be hiding in one of your bags or boxes. Place the two boxes (or bags) in front of the child and ask him to look for RED. When he peeks inside the box or bag and finds the red cellophane, ask him to take RED out. Tell him, "Good finding RED for me!" Now repeat the game with BLUE.

- When you are finished with the "looking" game, show your child how to wad the cellophane in his hands. See how much of the cellophane he can stuff into his closed fists!
- Ask your child to put RED and BLUE back into their containers. This is good fine motor practice as well as problem solving experience for your toddler. He may need to use his words to ask you for HELP.
- Show your child how when the red and blue cellophane are combined, the color PURPLE is produced.
- If your child has difficulty remembering which container holds red or is unable to discriminate between red and blue, position the container with red closer to the child and ask him to get RED. This is an example of *errorless*

---

* This bonus sign is found in the *Toddler Sing & Sign* Dictionary (page 207)

learning, where the child's correct response is made easier through proximity during his first opportunity to "show what he knows." As he begins to grasp color concepts, you can move the two choices closer together.

- You can also color code the containers so that your toddler can match the cellophane to the box or bag.

It is important to supervise children as they play with cellophane, and to keep this material away from the child's mouth.

♪ Birds of a Feather Color Collage

VOCABULARY PRACTICE: color words, **BIRD**

DEVELOPMENTAL BENEFITS: sensory exploration, fine-motor practice, creative expression

MATERIALS: bird pattern (see next page) copied on colored paper: blue, red, black, yellow; glue (liquid glue, glue stick, or homemade glue); small brush; a variety of items to glue on your "birds of a feather" color collages (scraps of wrapping paper, ribbon, fabric, yarn and felt, foil, leaves, marshmallows, tissue paper squares, dry cereal, gummy bears, feathers, cotton balls, elbow macaroni, stickers, buttons, etc.)

Note: Use caution and supervise your child closely while he works with these small items.

DIRECTIONS: Copy the bird pattern provided on a solid yellow piece of paper. You and your child are going to make a color collage using varied materials to decorate the bird pattern. You can help your child make small glue dots on the bird as you go, or help him use a small brush to paint the bird with glue. If you choose to help your child make glue dots to hold the collage materials, I find it helpful to repeat a phrase that Mrs. V., a kindergarten teacher, used with her students: "A dot is a lot." This helps him learn that only a small amount of glue is needed to adhere something to his page.

Once the glue is ready, provide your child with an assortment of yellow items to place on his yellow bird. Your child will love sticking things on his bird. Providing a variety of different items allows him an opportunity for sensory exploration with a variety of different textures. He will love feeling the difference between a squishy gummy bear and a hard piece of dry cereal. Talk about how the items feel, and stress their color. Express excitement about how

your child is decorating his YELLOW BIRD. Purposely show him an object that is a different color. Help him to see that it is different and doesn't belong on this color collage.

The next time your child makes a "birds of a feather" color collage, provide materials that are two different colors. Mix up items that are blue with items that are green. Help your child sort the materials and pick the ones to match his bird. As he becomes more proficient with his color sorting skills, do not sort the materials before gluing, and see if he is able to sort as he glues.

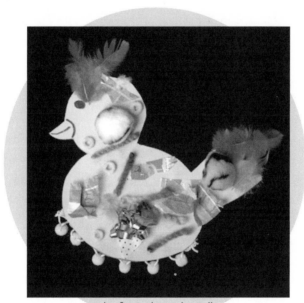

Birds of a Feather Color Collage

A SIGN OF SUCCESS

♪ A "DAD'S-EYE VIEW" OF *TODDLER SING & SIGN* ♪

Fathers have it rough.

Oh sure, our wives went through nine months of pregnancy, twenty-four hours of labor, and the agony of childbirth. But they have it easy when it comes to the ultimate challenge of parenthood: How do fathers connect with a baby who is a stranger to us?

A mother has a biological advantage in connecting with her child, an innate maternal instinct to care for him. Our baby grows inside her body. The baby is physically a part of the mother. After birth, the mother will spend countless hours breastfeeding to provide the proper nutrition and deepen the mother-child bond.

It isn't as easy for us fathers.

After a ten-hour workday, we come home hungry and tired, and often feel frustrated and alarmed by our lack of connection with Baby. We consider ourselves unnecessary to this new roommate who does nothing but eat, sleep, potty, and cry. It's not like we can go out to the backyard and toss the ball around yet. Heck, he doesn't even know who we are, since we're off at work all day. How are we to create any sort of meaningful relationship with him?

When my son Jackson was born, I decided to get involved. I changed his diapers. I sang and read to him. I kissed him, hugged him, and rolled on the floor with him. But whenever he wanted something, he would cry. His wails would ring in my ears. "What do you want?" I'd ask in frustration. "Tell me!" But he couldn't. It drove me crazy not knowing.

So I took Anne Meeker Miller's *Baby Sing & Sign* class.

> It's empowering to be able to communicate with your children. To see them learn the signs and tell you what they want is truly amazing.

Actually, it was my wife who suggested it. At first, I bristled at the suggestion. Why should we teach Jackson sign language? My son is not deaf. But I gave it a try, and it's one of the best things I ever did.

I was the only father in the class, but it didn't matter. I was singing loudly with the rest of the mothers, signing "more," "sit," "eat," "drink," and a dozen other words. The songs Anne sang stayed in my head. When I went home, I played her CD and practiced the signs with Jackson to his delight. Before long, something strange happened.

Jackson began using the signs I had taught him!

How exciting! He was learning! We could finally communicate! When he was hungry, instead of crying, he pointed to his mouth and I knew right away what he wanted. When he wanted to play, he gave me the "play" sign—which looks appropriately just like the gesture for "hang loose." When he was tired, he put his hand next to his ear for the "sleep" sign. Now that he is a toddler, he is using a variety of signs in combination with sounds and words to communicate what he wants and needs. *Toddler Sing & Sign* has helped us transition into the "Terrific Twos" with ease.

I know I'm not the only father who has benefited from the *Baby Sing & Sign* program. Bob Featherston's wife stayed home to raise their daughter, Lettie. She knew what all her cries meant. But when Bob came home from work, he had trouble understanding what his daughter wanted. So he read the *Baby Sing & Sign* book and joined his wife in using the techniques with his daughter. "The sign language allowed me to communicate at the same level as my wife," Bob said. "I wouldn't have to guess what Lettie wanted. She would just sign it."

Bob believes the sign language and music helped Lettie learn how to communicate faster than she would have otherwise. Plus, it brought him closer to his daughter. "The first time she signed 'love' showed me my effort to use sign language was completely worth every minute."

But without our wives' encouragement, would we really be doing *Toddler Sing & Sign?* John Young's wife introduced him to the program, and he thinks it made a huge difference in his two daughters' intelligence and happiness. "The idea of communicating basic wants, needs, and desires before they can speak made sense."

In fact, *Toddler Sing & Sign* has lessened the number of temper tantrums his daughters throw. One day when his wife ran into a friend at the store, "Hannah was growing tired of sitting in a shopping cart. Instead of screaming and throwing a fit, she just looked up at Melinda and kept signing 'all done.'"

Brad Hankins also signs with his two daughters and believes that without a father's support, the effort to teach sign language will fail. "It is important for both parents to be on board," he said. "If moms and dads are both signing with their child, the child is more likely to participate. The more a behavior is reinforced, the better it will be remembered."

Not only that, but Brad's oldest, Emery, adores Anne's music. She will play it in the kitchen as they sing and dance around her youngest sister, Rosie. "Sort of a 'Ring-Around-Our-Rosie' game," Brad says. "I am normally a shy and quiet guy, but I will act a little crazy for the sake of my children."

It's empowering to be able to communicate with your children. To see them learn the signs and tell you what they want is truly amazing. Fathers, trust me when I say there is no better way to create a lasting bond with your child than with *Toddler Sing & Sign*. The program helped me create a lasting bond with my son Jackson. He and I enjoy a "love affair" like no other as we sing, sign, and play each day.

We've made room in our family's game of "Ring-Around-the-Jackson" for one more playmate. Jackson's new baby brother, Alex, isn't old enough yet to walk in a circle on his own, but Daddy carries him as we play.

Toddler Sing & Sign is a family affair at our house—and DADDY is an enthusiastic participant!

—Matt Stewart, father

Matt and his toddler son, Jackson,
love to sing, sign, and play.

BOOKS TO READ

Most people know the time-honored rendition of the "Hush Little Baby" lullaby, complete with the promised purchase of a horse, cart, bull, and dog named Rover. Sylvia Long provides a new interpretation of *Hush Little Baby* (Chronicle Books), replacing all the things the parents might buy for the baby with memories they might share instead. The significance of this "lullaby lesson" will not be lost on your savvy little baby. Create some memories of your own as you sing the story to your toddler.

GOAT

Bill Grogan's Goat by Mary Ann Hoberman (Little, Brown Young Readers)

G Is for Goat by Patricia Polacco (Philomel)

Joey Goat by Barbara Derubertis (Kane Press)

The Three Billy Goats Gruff by Stephen Carpenter (HarperFestival)

Up Went the Goat by Barbara Gregorich (School Zone)

BULL/COW

Cows in the Kitchen by June Crebbin (Candlewick Press)

Kiss the Cow! by Phyllis Root and Will Hillenbrand (Walker Books)

The Cow That Went OINK by Bernard Most (Voyager Books)

There's a Cow in the Cabbage Patch by Clara Beaton and Stella Blackstone (Barefoot Books)

SWEET

Brown Sugar Babies by Charles R. Smith Jr. (Jump at the Sun)

Honey Baby Sugar Child by Alice Faye Duncan (Simon & Schuster Children's Publishing)

Sweet Baby Coming by Eloise Greenfield (HarperCollins Children's Books)

Sweet Dreams, Sam by Yves Got (Chronicle Books)

Sweet, Sweet Baby! by Javaka Steptoe (Cartwheel Books)

THE SAILING SHIP

ANIMAL WORDS TO LEARN: **MOUSE, DUCK**
OTHER WORDS TO LEARN: **SHIP/BOAT**
WORDS TO REVIEW: **HUG/LOVE, WHITE, FISH, FRIEND, PRETTY/BEAUTIFUL***
BONUS WORDS: **BACK*, NECK*, COOKIE*, APPLE*, WATER***

The original version of this chantey was sung by Hannah Louise Bishop to her young niece in the late 1800s. It is said that Ms. Bishop had a very beautiful singing voice, and that the song was passed down through the generations of her family as a lullaby. This new musical setting of "The Sailing Ship" includes some of the original lyrics of the Bishop family's lullaby. Dream well.

I saw a SHIP come sailing,	*Sign SHIP*
A sailing on the sea;	*Sign SHIP*
And it was deeply laden,	
With PRETTY things for me.	
With COOKIES in the cabin,	
And APPLES in the hold;	
The sails were made of silver silk,	*Sign SHIP*
The mast was solid gold.	*Sign SHIP*
The four and twenty sailors	
That stood beneath the deck,	
Were four and twenty WHITE MICE,	*Sign MOUSE*
With rings around their necks.	
The captain was a snow-WHITE DUCK,	*Sign DUCK*
With jewels on his back,	
And when this lovely SHIP set sail,	*Sign SHIP*
The captain, he said, "Quack, quack!"	*Sign DUCK*

* These bonus signs are found in the *Toddler Sing & Sign* Dictionary (page 207).

Sail [BOAT] on the silv'ry sea,   *Sign BOAT*
Hold on tight to me,   *Sign LOVE*
We can believe what we can dream!

I saw a SHIP come sailing,   *Sign SHIP*
With all the ones I adore,   *Sign LOVE*
And each and every person,
I couldn't fancy more.   *Sign LOVE*
We sailed into tomorrow,   *Sign SHIP*
Where FRIENDS we'll always be,
And we can dream as many dreams,
As FISHES in the sea.   *Sign FISH*
Oh, we can dream so many things,
For dreamers are we.

THE SAILING SHIP

Traditional / Adapted by Anne Meeker Miller

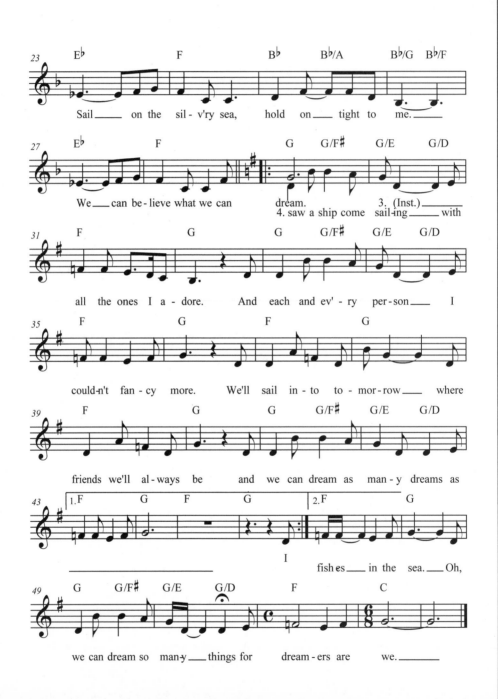

MOUSE

Brush one pointer finger across the tip of nose several times.

Child may place or tap pointer finger on nose.

DUCK

Open and close "duck's bill" next to mouth by tapping thumb to closed pointer and middle fingers.

Child may open and close *gathered fingertips* with or without placing them next to mouth, or place finger or fingers at mouth without making a motion.

SHIP/BOAT

Cup two *closed hands* together and move them forward as if floating in the water.

Child may place palms together and move them forward.

TIPS FOR INTRODUCING *THE SAILING SHIP*

○ The music CD of *Toddler Sing & Sign* contains ten songs. With each tune I created a "listening story" for you and your child. From the first song to the last, there are sounds for you and your child to listen to that involve you in the music: from the slamming drawers, clanging pots and pans, and noisy rooster in "All Around the Kitchen" to the creaking mast and ocean waves in "The Sailing Ship." Sign the sounds as they naturally occur in the music, and add a spoken prompt to direct your child's attention to the sounds they hear. For instance, sign ROOSTER as you say, "Did you hear the ROOSTER crowing?" when you listen to "All Around the Kitchen." You can also use signs to remind your child what comes next. For example, sign BOAT as you listen to the musical introduction of "The Sailing Ship." Your child may use the sign for BOAT to tell you that she likes that particular song and wants to hear it again.

○ Eager readers can see stories—characters, colors, actions, emotions—by reading the words on the page. I wanted to create a musical way for you and your child to interact with my "song stories" through sign and play. *Toddler Sing & Sign* provides multiple benefits for children, and the ability to imagine events and characters not present is yet another wonderful added attraction—and a valuable prereading skill.

○ When using American Sign Language (ASL) to communicate with a person, it is important to use signs that convey the true meaning of what we want to get across. For instance, when we sing "The Sailing Ship," we sing "all the ones I adore" and sign LOVE. The same is true for the phrase "I couldn't fancy more." The words of the phrase mean that we love someone. If you were to sign the ASL word for "fancy" instead, this would be confusing to a deaf child or adult. Consider this as you select words to teach your toddler. It isn't necessary to teach her several words when actually one word will convey the meaning best. Signing synonyms isn't necessary at this age and stage of your child's life.

♪ More Musical Fun with *The Sailing Ship*

● Butter tubs and milk jugs cut in half make wonderful boats for bath time. Let your child sail some of your plastic recyclables in your bathtub as she takes a relaxing bath before bedtime.

- Add blue food coloring to a bottle of water, seal the top securely, and show your child how to gently rock the bottle from side to side to view the "ocean waves." You can also make a sand shaker by putting sand and small seashells in a dry water bottle. Seal the top securely. Ask her WHAT? she sees inside the water bottle. Your sand play is practically as fun as a trip to the beach!

- Make a sailing ship out of a laundry basket. Have your toddler sit inside the basket. You may want to cushion the interior with a blanket or towel. Your sailor might also like a COOKIE or APPLE snack for her voyage or perhaps a flashlight to help navigate the ship. Push your toddler slowly around on the carpet as you sing "The Sailing Ship." Be careful not to make your little sailor seasick—especially right before bedtime. Your toddler may also like to just sit in her boat as she listens to the song. Quiet listening will help her hear the words of the song as well as the ocean waves and beautiful Scottish flute.

Travis keeps watch for "fish" as he sails
in his laundry basket "boat."

GAMES AND ACTIVITIES

♪ Colorful Sailor Cookies

VOCABULARY PRACTICE: color words, **COOKIE***

DEVELOPMENTAL BENEFITS: tactile sensory experience, fine-motor skills, color concepts

MATERIALS: prepared sugar cookie mix and all necessary ingredients for preparation, food coloring, one-gallon-size zipper bag

Colorful Sailor Cookies

DIRECTIONS: Combine all the necessary ingredients for the sugar cookie mix in the zipper bag. It would be wise to beat the eggs first before adding them to the mixture. Remove all air from the bag before zipping it closed. Place the bag on your child's highchair tray or a tabletop. Ask her to help make the cookies by pushing and mixing the dough. Show your child how to press the mixture within the bag with her palm and poke it with her fingers. You can work to mix the batter together.

To incorporate your color words, add food coloring to the batter in the bag. It will be fun to see how the batter changes as the food coloring is mixed into the dough. Tell your child you like the RED Sailor COOKIES she is creating! You can repeat the activity a different day with other colors. If you are feeling really fancy, you can add yellow and red food coloring to the batter to create ORANGE cookies. It will be fun to see how the separate colors combine in the batter to make a brand-new color.

It is best to leave the batter in the bag when adding food coloring for your child to mix, and to spoon the batter onto the cookie sheet. Food coloring can stain countertops as well as fingertips! A colorful alternative is to top your sugar cookies with colored sugar sprinkles. Spray the top of your cookies lightly with cooking spray and add the sugar sprinkles to create a colorful snack.

Be sure to share your cookies with others so that your child can describe them with her signs. Make a whole boatful of colorful cookies for your little sailor and her mates!

---

* This bonus sign is found in the *Toddler Sing & Sign* Dictionary (page 207).

♪ Mousie Menu

VOCABULARY PRACTICE: color words, **TRUCK, PLAY/TOY, BOAT, MOUSE, COOKIE**, APPLE*, CARROT***

DEVELOPMENTAL BENEFITS: using pictures to create meaning, using color words to describe objects, combining signs

MATERIALS: *If You Give a Mouse a Cookie* (book), trading card plastic protector sheet, index cards, pictures

DIRECTIONS: Find pictures representing several of the sign words taught in the *Toddler Sing & Sign* book, such as TRUCK, PLAY/TOY, or APPLE. Include a picture of a COOKIE—or CRACKER if you prefer to limit sugar at your household. You can also include words that have special meaning for your child. Signs for these words can be found using a sign language book or Web site video dictionary (see "References and Resources," page 223). Pictures can be cut from magazines or printed from images located using a Google image search. It might also be fun to take instant photos of objects to include in the book.

Mousie Menu

Cut out the pictures and paste them onto paper or index cards. Slip them into the pockets of a trading card plastic protector sheet. You can also use your computer to make a page that includes several different images and place this printed page in a plastic page protector.

Read Laura Joffe Numeroff's wonderful book *If You Give a Mouse a Cookie* (Laura Geringer/HarperFestival) to your child. Then show your child her Mousie Menu and ask her what else the mouse might want. She can point to other objects on the page and you can help her say and sign each of them.

You can make this a color activity by pairing the color and object words: "He would want a BROWN COOKIE, a YELLOW BOAT, an ORANGE CARROT. . . ." Another way to support age-appropriate reading skills is to help your child "read" the page by starting at the top left-hand corner of the page and reading straight across

---

* These bonus signs are found in the *Toddler Sing & Sign* Dictionary (page 207).

the page to the right. Then move down to the next line and repeat this process. Help your child point to each picture with her pointer finger to keep her place on the page.

♩ Rub-a-Dub-Dub—A Toddler in the Tub

VOCABULARY PRACTICE: SHIP/BOAT, MOUSE, DUCK, WHITE, YELLOW, FISH, WHAT, FRIEND, PRETTY/BEAUTIFUL*, COOKIE*, APPLE*, WATER*

DEVELOPMENTAL BENEFITS: sensory experience, relaxation, task completion and cleanup

MATERIALS: bath toys—funnel, scoop, plastic cup, ship/boat, washcloth, soap

After bath time with lots of "boats" and bubbles, it is smooth sailing into bed!

DIRECTIONS: "The Sailing Ship" is a great song to play at the conclusion of bath time. Play lullabies and other relaxing music while you help your child bathe. Let her play with her toys in the water while listening to the relaxing music.

When it is time for the bath to conclude, turn on the song "The Sailing Ship" as you tell your child that it is the last bath song. Sway slowly to the music as you and your child start to clean up the bath toys. Once the toys are picked up, use your hand or the washcloth to gently move the water to the rhythm of the song. Encourage your child to do the same. You can also rub the washcloth on her back or along her arms to the rhythm of the music.

Sign the words that you know as you hear them: SHIP, WATER, MOUSE, DUCK, WHITE, YELLOW, PRETTY, FRIEND, COOKIE, APPLE, FISH. You can make the signs in the water or out. Use a soft voice to sing along and talk to your child. Your soft voice and the slow, rhythmic tempo of the song will help signal to her that it is time to begin winding down in anticipation of sleep. "The Sailing Ship" will soon slumber. Sweet dreams!

---

* These bonus signs are found in the *Toddler Sing & Sign* Dictionary (page 207).

A SIGN OF SUCCESS

♪ BRIGHT-EYED AND BUSHY-TAILED: MAKE ♪ TIME FOR MUSICAL MEMORIES

"Well, my goodness, aren't you bright-eyed and bushy-tailed?" was one of my father's favorite greetings to me when I was a child. It meant "fired up and ready to go" and was just what I needed to skip out the door and embrace the day ahead at elementary school.

My father had great affection for all things musical. He taught himself to play the guitar and would play and sing the folk music of his favorite artists. We spent our summers canoeing the Current River in southern Missouri with a group of family friends, and would sing around the campfire late into the evening. Every new verse we children created for a folk song meant we got to stay up later, so we all took a turn.

My dad would bring his guitar along on our float trips. My sister and I knew we we would have to get ourselves to shore if our canoe capsized, because Dad would be too busy making sure his guitar didn't sink to the bottom of the river, while Mom swam our much-loved family mutt to shore, because, in her words, "The dog doesn't have a life jacket!"

The songwriter and folk musician Peggy Seeger wrote in *American Folksongs for Children:* "Folk songs are like the language from which they spring: rich and full of variety . . . Not only are these songs part of our history, but they are part of our present—they express things that will always be part of life, American Life."

Folk music is by its nature a work in progress. Just as stories change in the telling from generation to generation, so do folk songs. Before the time of sound recording, the only way that tunes could be taught was by singing them to one another. As parents or grandparents would teach a song to their young ones, they might make a new verse or change words to suit their fancy.

Folk songs are infinitely malleable, like precious metal always ready to be hammered or molded into something new. Adding or changing the lyrics of a folk song requires no specialized training. All that is necessary is a playful heart and a willingness to tap into your inner child in order to create a folk song that is uniquely your own.

I selected the songs for the *Toddler Sing & Sign* program in the hope that you and your

I selected the songs for the *Toddler Sing & Sign* program in the hope that you and your children will sing them with your hands and voices—and love them, as I do.

children will sing them with your hands and voices—and love them, as I do. Change the words, add verses, and make each of the songs your own. I am certain your children will teach them to their own babies someday.

My earnest wish is that you will continue to enjoy my "Bright-Eyed and Bushy-Tailed" tunes long after your children are able to speak in complete sentences and know all of their color and animal words by heart—even "chartreuse" and "aardvark."

Long may you sing (and sign!)

—Anne Meeker Miller

BOOKS TO READ

I don't easily succumb to the hypnotic power a book can elicit in readers large and small. Ever the analyst, I search for ways a book can educate as well as entertain my toddler friends. The illustrator David McPhail had me at "hello"—or "good night," as is the case with his bedtime book, *Wynken, Blynken, and Nod* (Cartwheel Books).

The poem was written by Eugene W. Field in 1889 on a piece of brown wrapping paper as he rode home on a streetcar. His three "fishermen" bunnies sail off into a magical world in a boat made of a wooden shoe. In combination with McPhail's luscious illustrations, this book makes my mouth water for a second serving. Pardon me while I leave you now so that I can read this book again from the beginning.

MOUSE

If You Give A Mouse a Cookie by Laura Joffe Numeroff (Laura Geringer/HarperFestival)

Mouse Paint by Ellen Stoll Walsh (Red Wagon Books)

Mouse Mess by Linnea Asplind Riley (Blue Sky Press)

The Best Mouse Cookie by Laura Joffe Numeroff (Laura Geringer Books)

The Little Mouse, the Red Ripe Strawberry, and the Big Hungry Bear by Don and Audrey Wood
  (Child's Play International)

DUCK

Duck on a Bike by David Shannon (Blue Sky Press)

Cold Little Duck, Duck, Duck by Lisa Westburg Peters (Greenwillow Books)

Farmer Duck by Martin Waddell (Candlewick Press

Five Little Ducks by Annie Kubler (Child's Play International)

One Duck Stuck by Phyllis Root (Candlewick Press)

SHIP/BOAT

Baby's Boat by Jeanne Titherington (Greenwillow Books)

Busy Boats by Tony Mitton (Kingfisher)

Little Bear's Little Boat by Eve Bunting (Clarion Books)

Row, Row, Row Your Boat by Annie Kubler (Child's Play International)

Ships and Boats by Peter Curry (Picture Lions)

TODDLER SING & SIGN DICTIONARY
CORE VOCABULARY WORDS

Gianni signs MOOSE.

ANIMAL SIGNS

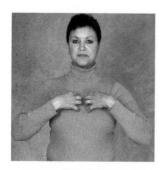

ANIMAL

BABOON

BEAR

BIRD

BULL

CAT

COW

CRAWDAD

DOG

DONKEY

DUCK

ELEPHANT

FISH

GIRAFFE

GOAT

HEN

HIPPO

HORSE

LAMB

LION

MONKEY

MOOSE

MOUSE

ROOSTER

SHEEP

TURTLE

ZEBRA

Tabitha signs GREEN.

COLOR SIGNS

BLACK

BLUE

BROWN

GRAY

GREEN

ORANGE

PINK

RED

WHITE

YELLOW

OTHER SIGNS

AFRAID

ALL DONE

ANGRY

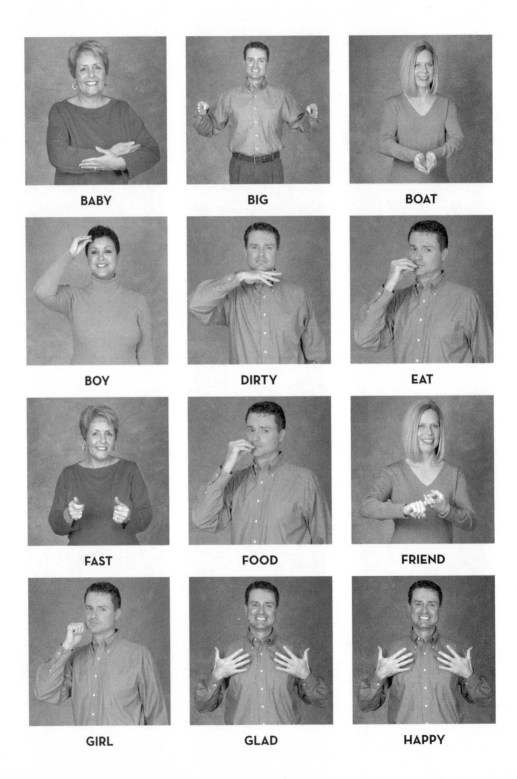

BABY	BIG	BOAT
BOY	DIRTY	EAT
FAST	FOOD	FRIEND
GIRL	GLAD	HAPPY

HIDE

HUG

HUSH

JUNGLE

LOOK

LOVE

MAD

MUD

MUSIC

PLAY

QUIET

SCARED

SEE

SHIP

SLEEP

SLOW

STOP

SUN

SWEET

TOY

TREES

TRUCK

WHAT?

TODDLER SING & SIGN
DICTIONARY
BONUS VOCABULARY WORDS

APPLE

Place curved pointer finger at cheek and twist forward.

BACK

Move *open hand* over shoulder and touch back.

BALL

Bring hands together to form shape of ball with *open cupped hands*.

BEAUTIFUL

Open hand moves in counterclockwise circle in front of face. Draw fingertips together during motion, and stop when in front of chin.

CAKE

Place fingertips of open *cupped hand* on upward palm of other hand. Lift *cupped hand* up as if cake is rising.

CARROT

Place *closed fist* with thumb on fingers at side of mouth and pretend to eat carrot.

CEREAL

Scoop one *cupped hand* across the other and up to mouth as if eating cereal from a bowl.

CHAIR

Form *two closed fingers* with both hands. Tap one on top of the other as if one hand "sits" on the other.

COOKIE

Place fingertips of *cupped hand* on upward palm of other hand. Twist back and forth as if cutting cookie dough.

DADDY

Place thumb of *open hand* on forehead.

DANCE

Swing *two open fingers* over other upward facing palm as if dancing back and forth.

EYES

Place pointer finger of one hand under eye, then move to other eye.

HAIR

Hold hair with pointer finger and thumb.

HELP

Place *closed fist* with thumb extended on other upward palm. Lift both hands together as if the bottom hand is lifting the other.

JUMP

Place *two open fingers* on the other upward palm, then curve fingers and move them up as if jumping.

KICK

Strike pointer finger of *closed hand* on the underside of other *closed hand* in a kicking motion.

KNEES

Place pointer finger of one hand on knee.

LAUGH

Place pointer fingers with extended thumb at each side of mouth. Brush up to show direction of smile.

LITTLE

Bring palms of *closed hands* close together as if showing a small size.

LOUD

Place pointer finger of *open hand* at ear, and then quickly move both *open hands* with palms down away from body.

MOMMY

Place thumb of *open hand* on chin.

MONSTER

Cupped hands above shoulders in imitation of monster.

NECK

Place pointer finger of one hand on neck.

PLEASE

Rub *open hand* on upper chest in circular motion.

PRETTY

Open hand moves in counterclockwise circle in front of face. Draw fingertips together during motion, and stop when in front of chin.

PURPLE

Place thumb between *two open fingers* and twist back and forth.

RUN

Pointer finger with thumb up hooks thumb of other hand. Move both hands forward.

SAD

Place two *open hands* in front of face with fingertips up. Draw hands in downward motion as if pulling sadness over the face.

SIT

Form *two closed fingers* with both hands. Tap one on top of the other as if one hand "sits" on the other.

SNEEZE

Place pointer finger of one hand across the upper lip under nose and pretend to sneeze.

STRUT

Downward facing *open hands* alternate forward as if they were feet walking.

TALK

Place pointer finger sideways at mouth and circle forward.

TOE

Place pointer finger of one hand at toe (or toe of shoe).

TOWN

Move arms in front of body from side to side while tapping fingertips of closed hands together, as if making rooftops.

TRAIN

Form *two closed fingers* palms down with both hands. Place one on top of the other and slide it back and forth.

VILLAGE

Move arms in front of body from side to side while tapping fingertips of closed hands together, as if making rooftops.

WAKE

Flick open thumb and pointer fingers placed at the corner of each eye as if eyes are opening.

WALK

Downward-facing *open hands* alternate forward as if they were feet walking.

WATER

Extend pointer, middle, and ring fingers of one hand. Place tip of pointer finger at side of mouth and tap.

GLOSSARY

AMERICAN SIGN LANGUAGE (ASL): widely accepted language of deaf culture utilizing gestures

APPROXIMATION: child's best effort to perform an action, such as imitating a sign, singing a song, or speaking a word

BALLAD: song that tells a story

CAREGIVER: person other than the parent who cares for children (e.g., sitter, other family member)

DEVELOPMENTALLY APPROPRIATE: skills or knowledge that fall within the range of what can typically be expected of someone at a certain age

ERRORLESS LEARNING: facilitating a child's correct response through proximity during her first opportunity to "show what she knows"

FINE-MOTOR MOVEMENT: actions of the muscles that control smaller, more isolated movements of the fingers and hands

FLUENCY: ability to maintain a steady pace and use inflection while reading, speaking, or singing

GROSS-MOTOR MOVEMENT: large-muscle movement of arms, legs, and torso

ICONIC LEARNING: using a sign to represent an object, idea, or concept

LEARNING CURVE: rate of progress for mastering or improving upon a skill

MOTOR PLANNING: ability to organize his or her motions in a purposeful way

PATTERNING: ability to add more objects or things in accordance with a design or plan after first observing the arranged sequence of objects or things

POSITIONAL CONCEPTS: concepts that identify where things are placed in relationship to a fixed object (e.g., off, on, around, under)

PRINT AWARENESS: ability to recognize that the print on the page actually represents spoken words

RHYMING: ability to recognize that single-syllable words start with different letter sounds, but sound the same at the end (e.g., beach and teach)

SEQUENCING: ability to order steps or arrange objects using a rule or pattern (e.g., smallest to largest)

TACTILE STIMULATION: feedback received from touch

VESTIBULAR STIMULATION: shifting of fluid in the inner ears, which influences a child's balance and coordination

VISUAL DISCRIMINATION: ability to determine visually subtle distinguishing characteristics among various objects or things

VOCABULARY: words a child knows or uses to express herself, including signed and spoken words

Isaac signs CAT.

REFERENCES AND RESOURCES

♪ Sign Language, Reading Readiness and Child Development

Acredolo, Linda, and Susan Goodwyn. *Baby Minds.* New York: Bantam Books, 2000.

Baby Signs. Chicago: Contemporary Books, 1996.

Apel, Ken, and Julie Masterson. *Beyond Baby Talk: From Sounds to Sentences, a Parent's Guide to Language Development.* Roseville: Prima Publishing, 2001.

Armstrong, Thomas. *In Their Own Way: Discovering and Encouraging Your Child's Multiple Intelligences.* New York: Tarcher, 2000.

Bahan, Ben, and Joe Dannis. *Signs for Me: Basic Sign Vocabulary for Children, Parents, and Teachers.* San Diego: Dawn Sign Press, 1990.

Bailey, Becky. *I Love You Rituals.* New York: Harper Paperbacks, 2000.

Baker, Pamela, and Patricia B. Bellen Gillen. *My First Book of Sign.* Washington, DC: Gallaudet University Press, 2002.

Cohen, Lawrence J. *Playful Parenting: A Bold New Way to Nurture.* New York: Ballantine, 2001.

Conkling, Winifred. *Smart-Wiring Your Baby's Brain: What You Can Do to Stimulate Your Child during the Critical First Three Years.* New York: HarperCollins, 2001.

Crain, William. *Reclaiming Childhood.* New York: Henry Holt, 2003.

Daniels, Marilyn. *Dancing with Words: Signing for Hearing Children's Literacy.* Westport, CT: Bergin and Garvey, 2001.

De Haan, Michelle. "Babies Recognize Faces Better than Adults." *BBC News: Health.* http://news.bbc.co.uk.

"Early Signs of Phobias in your Toddler." *Thelaboroflove.com.* http://www.thelaboroflove.com/articles/early-signs-of-phobias-in-your-toddler/.

Ezzo, Gary, and Anne Marie Ezzo. "Preschoolers and the Benefits of Play." *Growing Families International.* www.gfi.org.

Garcia, Joseph. *Sign with Your Baby: How to Communicate with Infants before They Can Speak.* Seattle, WA: Northlight Communications, 1999.

Gerber, Magda, and Allison Johnson. *Your Self-Confident Baby: How to Encourage Your Child's Natural Abilities from the Very Start.* John Wiley, 1998.

Goodwyn, Susan, and Linda Acredolo, "Encouraging Symbolic Gestures: Effects on the Relationship between Gesture and Speech." In J. Iverson and S. Goldin-Meadows, eds. *The Nature and Functions of Gesture in Children's Communication* (San Francisco: Jossey-Bass, 1998), 61–73.

Golinkoff, Roberta M., and Kathy Hirsh-Pasek. *How Babies Talk: The Magic and Mystery of Language in the First Three Years of Life.* New York: Penguin, 1999.

Gopnik, Alison, Andrew N. Meltoff, and Patricia Kuhl. *The Scientist in the Crib: What Early Learning Tells Us about the Mind.* New York: HarperCollins, 1999.

Hafer, Jan, Robert Wilson, and Paul Setzer. *Come Sign with Us: Sign Language Activities for Children.* Washington, DC: Gallaudet University Press, 2002.

Hanessian, Lu. *Let the Baby Drive: Navigating the Road of New Motherhood.* New York: St. Martin's, 2004.

Hart, Betty, and Todd Risley. *Meaningful Differences in the Everyday Lives of Children.* Baltimore: Brookes Publishing, 1995.

Hubert, Bill. *Bal-A-Vis-X: Rhythmic Balance/Auditory/Vision Exercises for Brain and Brain-Body Integration.* Wichita: Bal-A-Vis-X, 2001.

Karp, Harvey. *The Happiest Baby on the Block: The New Way to Calm Crying and Help Your Baby Sleep Longer.* New York: Bantam, 2002.

——— and Paula Spencer. *The Happiest Toddler on the Block: The New Way to Stop the Daily Battle of Wills and Raise a Secure and Well-Behaved One- to Four-Year-Old.* New York: Bantam, 2005.

Kumin, Libby. *Early Communication Skills for Children with Down Syndrome: A Guide for Parents and Professionals.* Bethesda, MD: Woodbine House, 2003.

McGuinness, Diane. *Growing a Reader from Birth: Your Child's Path from Language to Literacy.* New York: W. W. Norton, 2004.

Malley, Cathy. "Toddler Development." (Family Day Care Fact series) *National Network for Child Care.* Amherst: University of Massachusetts. www.nncc.org.

Mike, John. *Brilliant Babies, Powerful Adults: Awaken the Genius Within.* Clearwater, FL: Satori Press, 1997.

Miller, Anne Meeker. *Baby Sing & Sign: Communicate Early with Your Baby—Learning Signs the Fun Way through Music and Play.* New York: Marlowe and Company, 2006.

"NYU Neuroscientist Examines How Brain Responds to Fears That are Imagined and Anticipated, but Never Experienced." www.*Sciencedaily.com.*

Owens, Robert E., and Leah Feldon. *Help Your Baby Talk: Introducing the Shared Communication Method to Jump Start Language and Have a Smarter and Happier Baby.* New York: Berkley Publishing Group, 2004.

Paris, Eileen, and Thomas Paris. "Toddler Fears!" http://*Storknet.com.*

"Rockabye Baby: Research Shows Gentle Singing Soothes Sick Infants." www.*Sciencedaily.com.*

Pica, Rae. *A Running Start: How Play, Physical Activity, and Free Time Create a Successful Child.* New York: Marlowe and Company, 2007.

Rogers, Fred. *The World According to Mister Rogers: Important Things to Remember.* New York: Hyperion, 2003.

Schaefer, Charles E., and Theresa Foy DiGeronimo. *Ages and Stages: A Parent's Guide to Normal Childhood Development.* New York: John Wiley, 2000.

Schwartz, Sue, and Joan Heller Miller. *The New Language of Toys: Teaching Communication Skills to Children with Special Needs, A Guide for Parents and Teachers.* Bethesda, MD: Woodbine House, 2004.

Stipek, Deborah, and Kathy Seal. *Motivated Minds: Raising Children to Love Learning.* New York: Owl Books, 2001.

Rimm, Sylvia. *How to Parent So Children Will Learn.* Watertown, WI: Apple, 1990.

Rosenfeld, Alvin, and Nicole Wise. *Hyper-Parenting: Are You Hurting Your Child by Trying Too Hard?* New York: St. Martin's, 2000.

Rush, Kay. "Using Sign Language in High/Scope Programs." *High/Scope Extensions.* www.highscope.com, Summer 2005.

Schank, Roger. *Coloring Outside the Lines: Raising a Smarter Kid by Breaking All the Rules.* New York: HarperCollins, 2000.

Slier, Debby. *Animal Signs.* Washington, DC: Gallaudet University Press, 2002.

Stewart, David. *American Sign Language the Easy Way.* Hauppauge, NY: Barron's Educational Series, 1998.

Straub, Susan, and K. J. Dell'Antonia. *Reading with Babies, Toddlers, and Twos.* Naperville, IL: Sourcebooks, 2006.

Trelease, Jim. *The Read-Aloud Handbook,* 6th ed. New York: Penguin, 2006.

Trudo, Richard. "Helping Your Late-Talking Children." *Medicinenet.com.* http://www.medicinenet.com/script/main/art.asp?articlekey=52130.

Warburton, Karyn. *Baby Sign Language for Hearing Babies.* New York: Penguin, 2006.

Ward, Sally. *Baby Talk: Strengthen Your Child's Ability to Listen, Understand, and Communicate.* New York: Ballantine, 2001.

Whitehurst, Grover J., and Christopher J. Lonigan. "Emergent Literacy: Development from Prereaders to Readers." In *Handbook of Early Literacy Research,* Susan B. Neuman and David K. Dickinson, eds. New York: Guilford Press, 2002.

Avery signs ORANGE.

♪ Music for Young Children

Appleby, Amy, and Peter Pickow, eds. *The Library of Children's Song Classics.* New York: Amsco, 1993.

Bradford, Louise L., ed. *Sing It Yourself: 220 Pentatonic American Folk Songs.* Sherman Oaks, CA: Alfred Publishing, 1978.

Brown, Marc. *Hand Rhymes.* New York: Penguin, 1985.

Campbell, Don. *The Mozart Effect for Children: Awakening Your Child's Mind, Health, and Creativity with Music.* New York: HarperCollins, 2000.

Cole, William, ed. *Folk Songs of England, Ireland, Scotland, and Wales.* Garden City, NY: Doubleday, 1961.

Cromie, William J. "Mozart Effect Hits Sour Note." *Harvard University Gazette,* September 16, 1999. http://www.news.harvard.edu/gazette/1999/09.16/mozart.html.

Daniel, Mark. *A Child's Treasury of Poems.* New York: Dial, 1986.

Feieraband, John M. *The Book of Songs and Rhymes with Beat Motions: Let's Clap Our Hands Together.* Chicago: GIA Publications, 2004.

———. *The Book of Echo Songs.* Chicago: GIA Publications, 2003.

———. *The Book of Lullabies.* Chicago: GIA Steps, 2000.

———. *The Book of Simple Songs and Circles.* Chicago: GIA Steps, 2000.

————. *The Book of Tapping and Clapping.* Chicago: GIA Steps, 2000.

————. *The Book of Wiggles and Tickles.* Chicago: GIA Steps, 2000.

————. *Music for Very Little People.* New York: Boosey and Hawkes, 1986.

Fox, Dan. *A Treasury of Children's Songs: Forty Favorites to Sing and Play.* New York: Henry Holt, 2003.

————. *Go In and Out the Window: An Illustrated Songbook for Young People.* New York: Metropolitan Museum of Art: Henry Holt, 1987.

Fuller, Cheri. *How to Grow a Young Music Lover.* Colorado Springs: Waterbrook Press, 2002.

Glazer, Tom. *Music for Ones and Twos: Songs and Games for the Very Young Child.* New York: Doubleday, 1983.

Hale, Glorya. *An Illustrated Treasury of Read-Aloud Poems for Young People.* New York: Black Dog and Leventhal, 2003.

Kleiner, Lynn. *Jungle Beat.* Van Nuys, CA: Alfred Publishing, 2006.

————. *Kids Can Listen, Kids Can Move!* Van Nuys, CA: Alfred Publishing 2003.

————. *Toddlers Make Music! Ones and Twos! For Parents and Their Toddlers.* Van Nuys, CA: Alfred Publishing 2000.

————. *Kids Make Music! Twos and Threes! For Parents and Their Children.* Van Nuys, CA: Alfred Publishing 2000.

Langstaff, Nancy, and John Langstaff, eds. *Jim Along, Josie: A Collection of Folk Songs and Singing Games for Young Children.* New York: Harcourt Brace Jovanovich, 1970.

Lomax, John, and Alan Lomax, eds. *Best-Loved American Folk Songs.* New York: Grosset and Dunlap, 1947.

————. *Our Singing Country: Folk Songs and Ballads.* New York: Dover, 1941.

Orff-Schulwerk (American Edition). Volume 1. *Music for Children: Preschool.* Ed. Hermann Regner. Miami, FL: Schott Music, 1982.

Ortiz, John. *Nurturing Your Child with Music: How Sound Awareness Creates Happy, Smart, and Confident Children.* Hillsboro, OR: Beyond Words, 1999.

Piazza, Carolyn L. *Multiple Forms of Literacy: Teaching Literacy and the Arts.* Upper Saddle River, NJ: Prentice-Hall, 1999.

Rauscher, Frances H., Gordon L. Shaw, Linda J. Levine, and Katherine N. Ky. "Music and Spatial Task Performance: A Causal Relationship." Paper presented at the American Psychological Association 102nd Annual Convention, Los Angeles, California, 1994.

Rauscher, Frances H. "What Educators Must Learn from Science: The Case for Music in the Schools." In *Voice,* October 1995. www.wmea.org.

Sanders, Scott. *Hear the Wind Blow: American Folk Songs Retold.* New York: Bradbury Press, 1985.

Sandburg, Carl, ed. *The American Songbag.* New York: Harcourt, Brace, and World, 1927.

Seeger, Ruth Crawford, ed. *American Folk Songs for Children.* New York: Doubleday, 1948.

————. *Animal Folk Songs for Children.* Hamden, CT: Linnet Books, 1950.

Simon, William L., ed. *The Reader's Digest Children's Songbook.* Pleasantville, NY: Reader's Digest Association, 1985.

Spergler, Kenneth. *The Bear: An American Folk Song.* New York: Mondo Publishing, 2002.

Standley, Jayne, "The Power of Contingent Music for Infant Learning." *Bulletin of the Council for Research in Music Education* 147 (Spring 2001), 65–85.

The National Association for Music Education. *The School Music Program: A New Vision.* http://www.menc.org/publication/books/prek12st.html.

Trehub, Sandra E. "Musical Predispositions in Infancy." In *Annals of the New York Academy of Sciences* 930 (June 2001):1–16.

Winn, Marie, ed. *The Fireside Book of Children's Songs.* New York: Simon & Schuster, 1966.

♪ Web Sites

ABC Teach (www.abcteach.com/index.html)

Free content as well as additional fee-based content, including downloads of seasonal craft ideas and learning games.

A Basic Dictionary of ASL Terms. (www.masterstech-home.com/ASLDict.html)

A sign dictionary that features the videos from the Michigan State University Web site (along with additional signs) and descriptions of the signs to aid in memory.

American Baby. (www.americanbaby.com)

From the popular parenting magazine, information on parenting topics.

American Sign Language Browser (commtechlab.msu.edu/sites/aslweb/browser.htm)

This site provides hundreds of one-word video clips and instruction of ASL signs.

Baby Center (www.babycenter.com)

A site with a wide variety of resources on nearly every parenting topic from conception through childhood; also sells a range of products.

Baby Signs (www.babysigns.com)

The official site for Acredolo and Goodwyn's Baby Signs program.

Becky Bailey's Loving Guidance and Conscious Discipline Programs (www.becky bailey.com)

Information about the programs and products of Becky A. Bailey, PhD, the founder of Loving Guidance, Inc., a company dedicated to creating positive environments for children, families, schools, and businesses. Bailey is also the developer of the Conscious Discipline program.

Berkeley Parents Network (http://parents.berkeley.edu/advice/babies/signing.html)

Forum for parents to offer advice and comments about their experiences with baby sign.

Brain Connection (www.brainconnection.com)

An online source of information about the brain for educators, parents, students, and teachers.

Do 2 Learn. (www.d021earn.org)

Line drawings to use for picture schedules and important tasks like using the bathroom and washing hands.

EduScapes: A Site for Life-Long Learners of all Ages (www.eduscapes.com)

A potpourri of resources and topics for educators.

Handspeak (www.handspeak.com)

Information about baby sign is included at this site for learning visual languages.

John Feierabend's Early Childhood Music Program (www.giamusic.com)

Information about the philosophy, research, and teaching materials from one of the country's leaders in music for young children.

Kinder Signs: Baby Sign Language University (www.kindersigns.com)

An Orlando, Florida–based program founded by speech pathologist Diane Ryan devoted to teaching parents how to communicate with their babies before they can speak.

Love Language (www.lovelanguageforbabies.com or www.babysingandsign.com)

The official Web site for Baby Sing & Sign and the Kansas City–based Love Language program. Information about research, classes, and instructional products, as well as articles on getting started signing with babies. Song samples also available here.

Medline Plus (www.nlm.nih.gov/medlineplus/infantandtoddlerdevelopment.html)

Sponsored by the National Library of Medicine and the National Institutes of Health, this site provides links to articles and other sites on a wide variety of health, development, and general parenting information.

Music Rhapsody. (www.musicrhapsody.com)

Lynn Kleiner is founder and director of Music Rhapsody, a music program based in Manhattan Beach, California. This is one of the first programs in the nation specializing in music classes for young children. Their Web site offers information about classes and products.

Adelina signs HORSE.

My Baby Can Talk. (www.mybabycantalk.com)

Features information about signing with babies and children, as well as a nicely done video sign dictionary including hundreds of words frequently used with babies and toddlers.

National Institute of Environmental Health Sciences (NIEHS) Kids' Pages (www.niehs.nih.gov/kids)

A wonderful collection of resources for parents and educators, including an index with lyrics for hundreds of children's' songs. Many include a simple instrumental arrangement to help you learn or recall the melody.

Parenting (www.parenting.org)

Short, practical articles on a number of parenting topics for babies through adolescents.

Peggy Seeger (www.pegseeger.com)

Stories, humor, and information by Ms. Seeger about her experiences as a songwriter, singer, and member of the famous folksinging Seeger family. Family recordings from the Seeger family (Rounder Records) containing music collected by Ruth Crawford Seeger are also available here, including: American Folk Songs for Children, Animal Folk Songs for Children, *and* American Folk Songs for Christmas.

Public *Broadcasting* System. (www.pbs.org/parents)

Lots of information about parenting topics as well as information about their educational programming.

Real Families (www.real-families.com)

Laura Murphy, program founder, uses real-life examples and expectations to provide parenting, marriage, and family education. Classes and individual coaching are available.

Sign 2 Me (www.sign2me.com)

Information about Joseph Garcia's "Sign with Your Baby" program.

Signing Baby (www.signingbaby.com/main)

Created by a signing mother, this Web site includes articles, signing stories, and photographs of babies signing.

The Happiest Baby (www.thehappiestbaby.com/default.asp)

Dr. Harvey Karp is a nationally renowned expert on children's health and the environment. His Web site shares information about his techniques for living with and loving babies and toddlers, as well as information about his books and classes.

ABOUT THE AUTHOR

ANNE MEEKER MILLER, PhD, is the founder of the Love Language program. Through her writing and workshops, she shares information about the benefits of music, sign language, and play for infants and toddlers and gives easy and practical strategies for integrating all three into the daily lives of families.

Anne is a music therapist for the early childhood special education program of the Blue Valley School District in Overland Park, Kansas. Her preschool students were the inspiration for her work with sign language and music. Anne observed the positive impact song and sign had on the language skills of her students, and she wanted to have an even earlier influence in the lives of children when language is first acquired.

Anne has taught music to students from preschool through college levels. She received the Excellence in Teaching award given by the Learning Exchange, Kansas City Chamber of Commerce, and the *Kansas City Star.* She was a commission member of the Housewright Symposium on the Future of Music Education sponsored by the Music Educators National Conference.

She is the author of *Baby Sing & Sign: Communicate Early with Your Baby—Learning Signs the Fun Way through Music and Play* (Marlowe & Company, 2006). Her debut album, *Bright-Eyed and Bushy-Tailed,* won NAPPA and Parent's Choice Honors awards. She loves performing and has joined the band Konza Swamp for several concerts in the Kansas City area.

Anne lives in Olathe, Kansas, where she enjoys spending time with her husband, three sons—Greg, Kevin, and Andy—and their wheaten terrier. Her hobbies include laundry and carpooling.

CONTRIBUTORS

♪ Jennifer Ferguson

Jennifer was a preschool special education teacher for ten years. She received the Fox 4 News Crystal Apple award and the Excellence in Education award for her teaching contributions while with the Blue Valley School District in Overland Park, Kansas. Sign language, music, and movement activities were the cornerstones of her teaching in her preschool classroom. She is currently the *Baby Sing & Sign* national training director and teaches classes at two major medical centers in the Kansas City area. Jennifer has a special interest in the use of music and movement activities to enhance language and learning and has pursued research in this area. Jennifer attended the University of Kansas for both her undergraduate and graduate studies. She has a bachelor's degree in speech pathology and audiology and dual master's degrees in early childhood special education and early childhood deaf education.

Jennifer lives in Leawood, Kansas, with her husband, Aaron; toddler, Maizie; and two dachshunds. She enjoys cooking, decorating, and shopping for antiques, and most important, spending time with her family.

Jennifer created many of the games and activities for the book.

♪ Amy Scavuzzo

Amy Scavuzzo is a third-generation teacher and has taught kindergarten and first grade in the Blue Valley School District in Overland Park, Kansas. She observed the impact singing and signing had on her students' abilities to develop prereading skills. It was through her work as a classroom teacher that she became interested in the research supporting singing and signing with babies and toddlers. During her time as a classroom teacher she was a nominee for the Sallie Mae First Class Teacher award and was Blue River Elementary's Master Teacher nominee in 2003. A graduate of the University of Kansas with a degree in elementary education, Amy also earned her master's degree in curriculum and instruction.

Amy currently works as a parent educator for the Hickman Mills Parents as Teachers program and has taught *Baby Sing & Sign* classes as well. Amy is married to Santo and the proud mommy of Isabella and Gianni, both of whom are "graduates" of Anne Meeker Miller's *Baby Sing & Sign* program.

Amy created picture book lists and activities for the book.

♪ Kendall Burr

Kendall Burr has been a teacher of young children since her days at Nancy Stone's swimming school at age thirteen. Since that time, she has worked in early childhood as a preschool special education teacher, a special education consultant, a curriculum consultant, and is currently an early interventionist for infants and toddlers. She has degrees in early childhood education and early childhood special education, as well as work in educational administration. Born and raised in Iowa, Kendall attended the University of Northern Iowa and Iowa State University as well as Pittsburg State University in Kansas. She has been the recipient of a number of awards for her undergraduate and graduate work, and received a Teacher of the Year award from the Blue Valley School District in Overland Park, Kansas.

Kendall lives in Kansas City, Missouri, with her husband, Brad, where they sing and sign with their amazing toddler, Isaac; their fabulous baby, Avery; and even their affable mutt, Eddie—who has yet to sign back.

Kendall is the author of "Getting Ready for Preschool with *Toddler Sing & Sign*" (page 170).

♪ Matt Stewart

Matt Stewart currently works as an anchor/reporter for KCTV5 News in Kansas City, Missouri. Born and raised in Omaha, Matt graduated in 1997 with a degree in journalism from Northwestern University, where he played strong safety. The team won two Big Ten Championships and went to the Rose Bowl and Citrus Bowl. He and his wife, Christina, have two sons, Jackson and Alex. When not singing and signing with his sons—or report-ing the news—Matt spends time with his family and roots for the Huskers and Royals to win!

Matt is the author of "A Dad's-Eye View of *Toddler Sing & Sign*" (page 188).

♪ Jeff Petrie, illustrator

Jeff Petrie has been interested in drawing ever since he was a child. He studied graphic design at Johnson County Community College in Overland Park, Kansas. A piece of his artwork was featured at the Muscular Dystrophy Association national headquarters, and his Christmas card illustrations were chosen for the Muscular Dystrophy Association's Holiday Wishes Collection in 2000 and 2003. Jeff received the MDA Personal Achieve-ment award for the Kansas City area and the state of Kansas in 2001.

Jeff enjoys listening to and collecting music, going to concerts, surfing the Internet, and hanging out with friends. He lives in Overland Park, Kansas, with his family and two dogs, Einstein and Hailey. His whimsical illustrations are a wonderful addition to this book.

♪ Amy Martin, photographer

After a previous life as a computer software designer and several wonderful years at home raising her three beautiful daughters, Amy Martin decided to follow her passion and begin a new career as a portrait photographer. With the encouragement and support of her fam-ily and friends, she started a small studio in the Kansas City area, where she spends her time capturing the magic and innocence of small children. Amy's work was also featured in Anne Meeker Miller's *Baby Sing & Sign* book.

Amy lives in Olathe, Kansas, with her husband, daughters and a small menagerie of four-legged friends. Her photographs are a favorite feature of Miller's *Baby* and *Toddler Sing & Sign* books and capture the playfulness and fun we aspire to share with our readers.

ACKNOWLEDGMENTS

A STANDING OVATION to my consultants and "Miller's Angels": Kendall Burr, Jennifer Ferguson, and Amy Scavuzzo. I would still be spinning in a circle working on the table of contents if not for you. You have enriched my life and my book. A "shout out" to the parents and children of the Blue Valley School District and my *Baby/Toddler Sing & Sign* class participants.

I am grateful for Jim "Mr. Stinky Feet" Cosgrove, a man of unlimited talent and generosity, for lending his journalistic as well as musical talents to this book. Thanks to the following friends who jumped in and got their hands dirty doing any and all things necessary: Collette Barnes-Maelzer, Dr. Cindy Colwell, Dr. Alice-Ann Darrow, Jonann Ellner, Pola Firestone, Charles Golladay, Barb and Tony Harper, Brad and Megan Hankins, Jan Holthus, Dr. Kim Inks, Dr. Harvey Karp, Lynn Kleiner, Derek Martin, Dr. Marvalene Moore, Stephanie Parks, Dr. Dena Register, and Deb Webster.

Appreciation to my focus group: Melissa Anschutz, Genevieve Burt, Mandy Featherston, Megan Hankins, DeLynn Jenkins, Melissa Klusman, Mary Lee Leu, Rainey Rinaldi, Julie and Tim Steele, Myra Valdez, and Melinda Young.

Thanks to all of those whose photographs appear in the book: Avery, Kendall, and Isaac Burr; Marlin, Genevieve, and Tabitha Burt; Maia and Giao Carrico; Stephen Curnes; Avery, Eleanor, and Randy Erickson; Bob, Amanda, and Lettie Featherston; Maizie Ferguson; Austin, and Summer Gardner; Emery and Rosie Hankins; Maggie McKeown; Isabella and Gianni Scavuzzo; Jackson and Matt Stewart; Dana and Keaton Turner; Adelina and Myra Valdez; Beth, Chris, and Rachel Watts; Travis Webster; Matthew and Meganne Welchhans; and Elliana Wandick.

Bravo to my sign language models: Kellen Broeckelmann, Erin Burge, Jordan Clark, Major Copeland, Jennifer Ferguson, Kian Fogarty, John Hansen, Julia Masterson, Sheryl Porter, and Lillian Reed.

Thanks to all of my musical collaborators for their talent, creativity, energy, and willingness to work for minimum wage: Ian Demory, Teresa Murray, Mike Nicholis, and the Konza Swamp band—Chris DeVictor, Caleb Gardner, Nick Gardner, Jimmy Smith, Beth Watts, and Garrett White. Bravo to Jan Holthus for creating all the musical scores.

Heartfelt appreciation to Richard "Pixie Dust" McCroskey for all of his sweet bells and whistles. Thanks especially to "Big Time Producer" Rick Burch for being a part of my own personal miracle, and for his devotion to making wonderful music for little children. Your attention to detail at the molecular level is astonishing.

To my literary agent and wonderful friend Neil Salkind, I send a thank-you as tall and grandiose as the University of Kansas campanile. Thanks also to my editor, Katie McHugh, for channeling her inner speech and language pathologist to guide this project to fruition with affection and grace.

Hooray for my amazing husband, Dan, and our singing sons, Andy, Kevin, and Greg. Collectively you possess the brightest eyes and bushiest set of tails I have ever had the good fortune to encounter. I love you more than a million Table Rock Lakes.

Thanks to my father for a lifetime of memories and for giving me a sister named Donna, whom I tolerated for the first twenty years of my life and have adored for the remainder.

—AMM

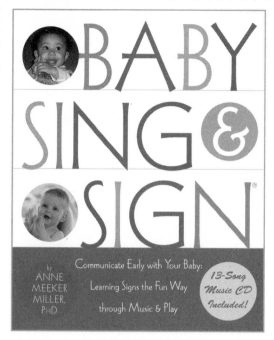

BRIGHT-EYED AND BUSHY-TAILED
MUSIC CD

1. ALL AROUND THE KITCHEN
(Traditional / Adapted by Anne Meeker Miller)

2. GRIZZLY BEAR
(Traditional / Adapted by Anne Meeker Miller)

3. THE CRAWDAD SONG
(Traditional / Adapted by Anne Meeker Miller)

4. TINGALAYO
(Traditional / Adapted by Anne Meeker Miller)

5. DOWN ON GRANDPA'S FARM
(Traditional / Adapted by Anne Meeker Miller)

6. I'M A TURTLE
(Lyrics and Music by Charles Golladay © 2006. Permission secured. All rights reserved.)

7. THE ANIMAL FAIR
(Traditional / Adapted by Anne Meeker Miller)

8. THE LION SLEEPS TONIGHT (WIMOWEH)
*(Based on a song by Solomon Linda and Paul Campbell.
Lyrics by George David Weiss, Hugo Peretti, and
Luigi Creatore. © 1961, renewed Abilene Music,
LLC. Permission secured. All rights reserved.)*

9. THE MOCKINGBIRD
(Traditional / Adapted by Anne Meeker Miller and Jeff Martin)

10. THE SAILING SHIP
(Traditional / Adapted by Anne Meeker Miller)

Produced by Anne Meeker Miller and Rick Burch
Engineered by Rick Burch/KC Creative Media
Mixed by Rick Burch
Mastered by Richard McCroskey
VOCALS: Anne Meeker Miller, Rick Burch,
Jim "Mr. Stinky Feet" Cosgrove, Lana
Herman, Beth Watts, and Garrett White
GUITAR: Richard McCroskey and Garrett White
BASS: Rick Burch and Chris DeVictor
RHYTHM: Mike Nicholis

BANJO: Nick Gardner
MANDOLIN: Caleb Gardner
SLIDE GUITAR: Jimmy Campbell
CHILDREN'S CHORUS: Shannon Dunaway, Nicole
Fugit, Macy Gosselaar, Kala Holder, and
Andrea Strickler
CHORUS DIRECTOR: Teresa Murray
OTHER INSTRUMENTALS: Richard McCroskey and
Rick Burch
PIXIE DUST: Richard McCroskey